Future Trends

Future Trends

A Guide to Decision Making and Leadership in Business

Lawrence R. Samuel

ROWMAN & LITTLEFIELD
Lanham • Boulder • New York • London

Pages 3–7 of the Introduction were originally published in Lawrence R. Samuel, *Future: A Recent History* (Austin: University of Texas Press, 2009), 1–6.

Published by Rowman & Littlefield
A wholly owned subsidiary of The Rowman & Littlefield Publishing Group, Inc.
4501 Forbes Boulevard, Suite 200, Lanham, Maryland 20706
www.rowman.com

Unit A, Whitacre Mews, 26-34 Stannary Street, London SE11 4AB

British Library Cataloguing in Publication Information Available

Library of Congress Cataloging-in-Publication Data

Names: Samuel, Lawrence R., author.
Title: Future trends : a guide to decision making and leadership in business
/ Lawrence R. Samuel.
Description: Lanham : Rowman & Littlefield, [2018] | Includes bibliographical
references and index.
Identifiers: LCCN 2017058540 (print) | LCCN 2017060090 (ebook) | ISBN
9781538110362 (electronic) | ISBN 9781538110355 (cloth : alk. paper)
Subjects: LCSH: Business forecasting. | Leadership. | Decision making.
Classification: LCC HD30.27 (ebook) | LCC HD30.27 .S26 2018 (print) | DDC
658.4/03—dc23
LC record available at https://lccn.loc.gov/2017058540

♾️™ The paper used in this publication meets the minimum requirements of
American National Standard for Information Sciences—Permanence of Paper
for Printed Library Materials, ANSI/NISO Z39.48-1992.

Printed in the United States of America

~

Contents

~

Introduction

Welcome to the future, or at least a big part of it. *Future Trends: A Guide to Decision Making and Leadership in Business* is designed to help you be in the right place at the right time with the right ideas. By identifying sixty global, long-term trends and detailing how businesspeople can leverage them through short- and long-range thinking, the book is intended to serve as a powerful and practical body of knowledge. A major goal of *Future Trends* is to help you be a thought leader in your respective field. Thought leadership—having an informed opinion, demonstrating expertise in a particular subject, and serving as an agent of change within one's industry—is understandably much pursued in the business community, something on which this book intends to fully capitalize. Insight into the future is the ultimate form of thought leadership, I propose, reason enough that the book should prove to be a useful resource. In a nutshell, this book will offer you a new vocabulary or language to speak in the marketplace and show you how to apply these conversation skills to your particular business or endeavor. By becoming more fluent in the future, readers will have a greater chance of being recognized as a trusted source and "go-to" person in their field, a valuable proposition.

    Future Trends is divided into six sections: Cultural Trends, Economic Trends, Political Trends, Social Trends, Scientific Trends, and Technological Trends. Each section includes ten trends that indicate where the world is heading. Many futurists focus on technology, ignoring the fact that the ways in which people actually live their lives are shaped by many other factors. The book thus takes a 360-degree, holistic view of tomorrow, offering readers a fuller understanding of life on earth over the next couple of decades. And rather than pursue a particular agenda—another common feature in futurism—*Future Trends* consists of a carefully curated collection of those trends that I believe are most relevant and meaningful for businesspeople.

It is the translation of the sixty Future Trends, however, where I believe *Future Trends* most stands out. Businesspeople typically have to go through a time- and cost-intensive process to develop a decision-making and leadership platform, and then embark on another round of planning to put that platform into actual practice. Via a correlative set of a dozen implications and opportunities, the book shows how each Future Trend can serve as a foundation for strategic thinking, and how those platforms can be applied in real business settings. Translating the future into meaningful and relevant terms is the key to forward-looking decision making and leadership. Readers should apply their own industry, product or service category, and brand dynamics into the equation, however; this last step is the best way to generate actionable, implementable ideas for a specific business.

Importantly, by focusing on the long term, *Future Trends* avoids the main problem with most trend-oriented books: datedness. The book steers clear of here-today-gone-tomorrow things and experiences that compose most glimpses into the emerging cultural landscape. There is no mention of "what's in" or "what's out"; such short-term thinking has little relevance to sustainable decision making and leadership. Relatedly, viewing the trend universe from a global perspective eschews the narrow, Americentric nature of most sources aimed at a business audience, and the book's grounding in reality offers more practicality than that brand of futurism posing wild hypotheticals. More than ever, being in the right place at the right time with the right ideas requires having a vision of what likely lies ahead for the next decade or two on a global basis, something *Future Trends* is equipped to do. As well, most of the following Future Trends are situated within a historical context, an extremely helpful device that better futurists employ when extending trajectories.

Finally, another way that *Future Trends* skirts being instantly dated is by focusing on what is driving the trends versus the trends themselves. Many people, even managers, believe trends to be about the latest, the hippest, and the coolest, when in truth they have little or nothing to do with the fashion, hairstyle, band, or drink of the moment. (If something is "trending now," you can be sure it's not a real trend.) Actual trends—particular expressions or articulations of a society's values that are in ascent, that is, rising in popularity, status, worth, and power—reveal the seminal patterns or themes of society, telling us where it is headed and what it aspires to become. To that point, rather than being "trends for trend's sake," *Future Trends* parses or decodes the fundamental qualities or building blocks of each of the sixty trends included in the book. The result is a much more useful and relevant body of work that readers will be able to apply in their decision-making and leadership process for years to come.

"Every present is great with the future," wrote the German mathematician and philosopher Gottfried Leibniz in 1703, explaining why most of us, especially those in the world of business, are so interested in what is likely to come next. It should hardly come as news that the future (i.e., that which is yet to be) has always been viewed as a highly charged cultural site loaded with significance and meaning. The future, David Remnick explained in 1997, consists of "stories we tell to amaze ourselves, to give hope to the desperate, to jolt the complacent," implying that thinking about tomorrow really serves the needs of today. The future is indeed "always about the present," Remnick continued, a catharsis for "what confuses us, what we desire, what we fear."[1] Likewise, "prophecies and predictions tell us little or nothing about what will happen," David A. Wilson argues in his History of the Future, but rather "tell us a great deal about the fears, hopes, desires, and circumstances of the people who peer into their own future and imagine what it will be like."[2]

More than this, however, futurism (the practice dedicated to anticipating the future) is often propagandist, a cause attached to whatever, whenever, and however is being predicted. Just as history is "written by the winners," as the popular phrase goes, official versions of the future also carry an agenda and, at times, serve as a kind of political act. With many (actually an infinite number of) futures to choose from, prediction is thus typically not a random exercise but more often an attempt to turn a particular scenario into reality. And while symbiotically connected and codependent, the future and futurism can of course be going in separate directions, the two concepts in fact often sharing an inverse relationship. Positive views of the future do not imply a positive state of futurism, in other words, the latter enjoying some of its best days during the darkest days of the former. Concern and fears about the future unsurprisingly spark a greater demand for futurism, this accounting for the field's popularity during the economically depressed 1930s, the paranoid 1950s, and the self-loathing 1970s.

It is the pure unknowability of the future, however, that has made it such a powerful force in our imaginations and daily lives. "The future: have any two words excited more hope, prompted more dreams and visions?" asked William A. Henry III in 1992; the limitless possibilities of tomorrow are at the core of the visceral response those two words elicit.[3] Our pervasive interest in the future—whether it's reading one's horoscope in the daily newspaper, watching the weather forecast on the local news, betting on a ballgame, or subscribing to Bloomberg to get the inside scoop on what the stock market might or might not do—reflects our common desire to know the unknowable in order to anticipate it or, even better, control it. "The itch to know what's going to happen next seems engrained in modern man," Thomas Griffith observed in 1979, all of us competing with each other in what could be viewed as a marketplace of potential futures.[4] The survival of any species is in fact a kind of leap of faith in tomorrow, as the idea of the future is firmly entrenched in the act of creation. "Every garden and child is an expressed belief in the future," Stefan Kanfer wrote in 1976, the origins of life itself grounded in a commitment to the yet-to-be.[5]

While "to be human is to ponder the future," as David Rejeski and Robert L. Olson succinctly put it in 2006, actually knowing what's to come is of course impossible.[6] Like Oakland for Gertrude Stein, there's no "there" there when it comes to the future, a new horizon always appearing as soon as you reach the last one. It is, though, this inherent elusive and ephemeral quality of futurism that makes it so compelling, not unlike the thought of peering into Pandora's box to see what forbidden goodies might be inside. "It [the future] is more creative, more beautiful and strange than can be imagined by the past," Lewis Lapham mused in 1979, seconded by James Poniewozik's view a quarter century later that "nothing is more shimmeringly beautiful than the next big thing in our imagination."[7] That major world events have been considerably shaped by factors impossible to predict—insanity, genius, randomness—as Nassim Nicholas Taleb convincingly argued in his 2007 *The Black Swan: The Impact of the Highly Improbable*, attempting to know the future is only that much more desirable, one of our most powerful fantasies.[8]

Besides being an inherently losing proposition, it hasn't helped that more than one charlatan has hung out a futurist shingle, interested only in telling people what they want (or don't want) to hear to make a buck. Whether populated by those with alleged special powers—soothsayers, oracles, crystal ball gazers, clairvoyants, palm readers, dream interpreters, stargazers, and the occasional witch—or professional futurists with reams of "data" up their sleeves, the field has always been viewed as a bit shady, some considering the whole enterprise plain quackery. "To talk about history, you have to have your facts in order, but, to talk about the future, all you have to do is say you work in research," complained George F. Mechlin in 1983, a typical sentiment among the more skeptical.[9] A dozen years later, David Bouchier griped that, "financial advisers, think tanks, opinion polls, market researchers, the Federal Reserve and the CIA all specialize in getting the future completely wrong at enormous cost," he of the opinion that, "only mothers really know the future." "But the world pays no attention to mothers," Bouchier grumbled, "the world wants to hear the bad news from a genuine prophet with a long white beard."[10]

Even some genuine prophets, long white beard notwithstanding, regretted their career choice and felt they might be better off with a "real" job. "How did I ever get into the predicting business?" asked one of the best, Isaac Asimov, at the top of his game in the mid-1960s; he was convinced that "predicting the future is a hopeless, thankless task, with ridicule to begin with and, all too often, scorn to end with."[11] While he had a legitimate point, Asimov was actually overestimating how much the public (especially Americans) have looked back to see if prognosticators were right or wrong. And although critics have indeed often treated futurists with little respect, they have on occasion received the credit they richly deserve. "We desperately need prophets, even false ones, to help us narrow the infinity of plausible futures down to one or at least to a manageable handful," thought Lev Grossman in 2004, a refreshing take on those treading in tomorrow's waters. "They are our advance scouts, infiltrating the undiscovered country, stealing over the border to bring back priceless reconnaissance maps of the world to come," Grossman continued, an all-too-rare expression of appreciation for futurists.[12]

The ambivalence surrounding futurists and the field itself reflects the fact that its history has been a polarized one, with the world of tomorrow often imagined in utopian or dystopian language and imagery. If not a Rousseau-like peaceful kingdom where we all will one day live happily ever after, the future is frequently a place of impending catastrophe or, just as often, one in which the individual will be crushed under the foot of a totalitarian regime. The future has served as an opportunity to both vent our worst fears and air our greatest hopes, the most profound of the latter being that we'll live on after our bodies die. The notion of an afterlife—the core of many religions—is futurism in its purest form, with tomorrow conceived not as a place made much better by the next great invention or much worse by an alien invasion but as an alternative universe with its own rules. Futurism has always carried with it a sense of mystery, the ability to know the unknown deemed limited to those with special and, sometimes, evil powers. Prophets were, centuries ago, considered divinely anointed in some way, the strange art seen as common to members of certain families who possessed a genetic predisposition for it.[13]

This off-the-beaten-track aspect of futurism can be most readily seen within science fiction, the primary launching pad of twisted tomorrows over the last century. The standard tools of the sci-fi trade have served as some of the most familiar tropes of futurism not just as an entertaining diversion but as a way to safely contain the darkest sides of our imaginations. Mad scientists, master races, mutation, barbarism, and disembodied heads are just a few scenarios of future-gone-bad, most of these kinds of narratives not much more meaningful than that found in your typical horror movie of the week. The granddaddy of dystopia, however, is the creation of machines more intelligent or powerful than ourselves, this one reflecting our real-life (and, according to some current futurists, justifiable) fear of technology run amok. Not surprisingly, then, the robot or automatic man has been a ubiquitous figure in futurism, both appealing to our quest for perfection and acknowledging the threat that we may lose the essence of what makes us human.

The elephant in the futuristic room, however, has undoubtedly been our on-again, off-again relationship with science and technology. Since the Renaissance, in fact, science and technology have dominated our visions of tomorrow, our common dream to, as one mid-twentieth-century futurist put it, go where no man has gone before. Flying machines have been, of course, a staple of futurism, this despite the sensible argument within much of the day's scientific community that they would never get off the ground (the internal combustion engine was never really anticipated, even by the genius of the millennium, da Vinci). Time machines also have been commonplace in narratives of the future, these too believed by most to defy the laws of the physical universe (until relatively recently, when travel through time, at least backward, is considered possible, according to some string theorists).[14]

Overall, however, the actual pace of technology has almost always surpassed that expected by those peering into the future, the quantum leaps made possible by a new discovery impossible to anticipate. In his 1898 *The Sleeper Awakes*, for example, H. G. Wells nailed a number of technologies that were to be—radio, movies, air conditioning—but underestimated how quickly they would appear—about forty years instead of his projected two hundred.[15] Wells, who British "alternate history" novelist Harry Harrison credits with having created almost all themes of science fiction in his own "scientific romances," was off by almost a century when it came to man's landing on the moon, analogous perhaps to how futurists of the twentieth century missed the rapid evolution of information technology by a country mile.[16] Even more than overshooting technological achievements, however, it has been futurists' failure to anticipate major social change, most egregiously the women's rights and civil rights movements of the twentieth century, that has most seriously and justifiably damaged the reputation of the field. The bias toward predicting technological versus social progress has been and continues to be the Achilles' heel of futurism, with the next wave of gadgets and gizmos easier to see coming than a cultural tsunami. It is, as Arnold Toynbee has pointed out, ideas, not technology, that have stirred the biggest changes in history, something that more futurists could and should have taken to heart.

As you're now no doubt already aware, this is a different kind of business book. Most business books are just about business, which I believe is the wrong way to go about it. Business is usually the easy part, as, after all, that is what businesspeople do for a living. The more challenging piece of the equation is figuring out where one's business resides within the current and emerging cultural landscape and, even more challenging, deciding where it should go next. Learning from stories of success (and failure) through a case study approach is all well and good, but it's much too narrow a lens through which to view brands, consumers, and, most of all, the future. If one's mission is to infuse innovation and inspiration into one's business, which it should be, one has to look beyond what other businesses are or are not doing. The most successful companies, in fact, are those that look not to what other companies are doing but to what they should be doing based on emerging trends.

To that point, a big reason I wrote *Future Trends* was to pass on my learning from my years as a leading trend consultant to Fortune 500 companies and major ad agencies. Since 1990, I've taken a cultural approach to consumer insight that is designed to complement traditional (quantitative and qualitative) marketing research, a methodology grounded in the idea that the marketplace demands new and different kinds of research tools. Rather than what people say, think, or say they think—the focus of attitude-based, opinion-oriented traditional market research—it is only what people do that really matters, I hold; hence the reason for an anthropological approach. This kind of research is exactly what's needed to understand the consumer of both today and tomorrow, I firmly believe, something more businesspeople are realizing. While my competitors thus lead their focus groups and do their surveys, I focus on consumers' behavioral "paper trail" in order to identify innovative, culturally in-synch marketing opportunities. Via full immersion in what consumers do and are likely to do in the future, my approach reveals consumers' "passion points"—the key to creating compelling products, services, and communications.

The best way to use this book is to consider each of the sixty Future Trends within the context of your brand, company, category, and industry. By using just a single word to describe each Future Trend, I've consciously tried to avoid the kind of jargon that is typical in the trend and futurism space.

Pay special attention to those Future Trends in which there is some overlap (Microbranding and Grassroots, for example); that indicates that there is particularly rich territory to mine. Don't fret about a seemingly contradictory or paradoxical combination of Future Trends (Analog and Automation, say, or Individualism and Connectedness); trends often operate in juxtaposition to each other. Use the Decision-Making and Leadership Platform at the end of each Future Trend as an illustration of how to translate the information into actionable ideas. Think of them as fodder to create your own new business, strategic planning, new product, positioning, advertising, promotion, public relation ideas based on your own corporate mission, company assets, brand equities, and marketing initiatives. Again, welcome to the future!

CHAPTER ONE

~

Cultural Trends

Where does one begin to tell the story of the future? By taking a bird's eye view of emerging attitudes and behavior around the world, and then extending that outlook as far as it can reasonably go. Cultural trends represent the biggest landmarks, and thus serve as the logical place to get one's bearings before exploring the more detailed topography of tomorrow. As the broadest and deepest indicators of global values at any given time, cultural trends are our most useful guide to the economic, political, social, scientific, and technological landscape that looms ahead. Cultural trends are, in other words, about the big stuff—mega (and meta) markers that define who we are as a species and where we are likely to be headed in the future. From individualism to wisdom, androgyny to pharmacopeia, the trends that are most changing in global culture right now speak volumes for the future. Learning how to read, interpret, and harness the messages inherent in these changes is imperative for all leaders.

So what does our mile-high look-see tell us? First and foremost, that it's a very good time for an individual to be alive. In no previous period of history has there been a greater opportunity for a human being to realize his or her full potential, a wonderful thing given the repression and oppression of the self that was commonplace throughout the past few millennia. The world may be an increasingly scary place, as chapter 3 painfully shows, but there has never been a better chance for a person to define and achieve whatever it is he or she wants to do with the short time we have on the planet. The draconian restrictions placed on ordinary folk by large and powerful institutions continue to crumble, a lengthy process that was kicked into gear by the revolutions of the eighteenth century. The ability to make one's own decisions in life may be taken for granted but should not be underestimated; we are only now reaping the rewards of not having to pay heed to a relatively few people telling us what to do.

Is life in the still early part of the twenty-first century a piece of cake? Hardly. With greater autonomy and self-rule has come a heavy price—the pressure to do things on our own and ultimately determine our own fate. It is increasingly incumbent upon individuals to make their own mark, not an easy thing with seven and a half billion other potential competitors. The new boss is no longer the same as the old boss, a shifting of the existential plates that carries major consequences for people and organizations trying to find a place in the global economy. As well, speed and stress have become major signs of the times that add to the emotional cost of being alive in the third millennium.

As always, however, people are adapting to their cultural climate. Many are finding creative ways to do with less, and discovering a better quality of life in the process. Stripping away the layers of excess and carrying less overhead is a defining feature of our leaner and meaner times, something that presents significant challenges and opportunities in the world of business. Exponential change is (ironically) informing the present with a new kind of urgency, this too of great importance to those trying to sell something to someone. Consumers are asking not just "What's in it for me?" but "What's in it for me now?"—a question managers had better have an answer to. Along with consumers' greater demands and expectations has come an ability to alter their minds, bodies, and even spirits at a moment's notice. With the postmodern grab bag of identities from which to choose, consumers are in a nearly constant state of flux, making them a moving target difficult to reach, much less persuade. Needless to say, these ten cultural trends suggest that the future will be interesting times indeed for businesses of all kinds.

Future Trend 1: Individualism

Almost half a century after the "Me Generation" made headlines with its focus on the self, individualism is well on the way to becoming one of the central themes of the twenty-first century. Baby boomers did indeed look out for #1 in the hedonistic, therapeutic 1970s, but now individualism—acting in one's own interests versus those of an organized group or government—is arguably the guiding principle of our times. It's important to remember that from a historical view the idea and practice of individualism is a radical concept. The Enlightenment ideals of the eighteenth century were in opposition to the all-encompassing power of church and state that had endured for a millennium, and laid the seeds for the continual ascent of individualism over the past few hundred years.

Today, expressions of individualism are everywhere you look, making the me-ness of the "Me Generation" look comparatively mild. Living alone is no longer seen as odd or peculiar, for example, and usage of the words "I" or "me" in both verbal and written communication is significantly higher than in the past.[1] (It is the "selfie," however, that serves as the poster child for contemporary individualism.) The rise of individualism has run on a parallel course with a loss of faith and trust in large institutions, with this way of seeing the world showing no signs of reversing. In fact, there are clear signs that individualism is evolving into a global movement, as people all over the world rebuff external control in favor of sovereignty of the self. "Day by day, week by week, year by year we are experiencing a gradual but pervasive spread of individual autonomy and increasing confidence in personal judgment," wrote Jay Ogilvy for stratfor.com, seeing this as "for the most part, a good thing."[2]

In the United States, the embrace of individualism certainly relates to the decline of political partisanship and correlative rise of self-declared independents. (Much is made of the alleged great divide between Republicans and Democrats, but in fact the political landscape is more defined by citizens' individual stances on issues.) Likewise, the falling off of organized religion and interest in exploring personalized forms of spirituality reflect the rejection of institutional authority and affirmation of the self. And as Moises Naim argues in his *The End of Power*, the middle-classing of many nations and a more mobile world are contributing to a pervasive ethos of individuality. "When people are living fuller lives, they become more difficult to regiment and control," Naim wrote in the book, thus erosion of official power and escalation of self-rule is likely to accelerate in the future.[3]

For the business world, the triumph of individualism represents the permanent retirement of the "mass market" that served corporations for so long. If individualism is really about freedom and having choices in life, it's in the best interests of all kinds of organizations to view consumers or constituents as unique individuals rather than as belonging to a socially constructed group or really any form of "market." "The increased respect for self-reliance, democracy and individual freedoms has developed a culture of 'me first,'" the smart folks at UK-based Trend Monitor observed, "creating a more engaged, confident and vocal consumer and forcing companies and brands to re-assess the way they build relationships and interact with their customers."[4] Personalized products and services would be the most obvious strategic route to capitalize on individualism, but simply treating people as, well, people also makes a lot of sense in taking advantage of this first Future Trend.

Future Trend 1: Individualism

Decision-Making and Leadership Platform

Implications
The ethos of individualism is continuing to rise around the world.

- Individualism is becoming more extreme in developed nations and is taking root in developing ones.

Millennials' passion for individualism is well surpassing that of baby boomers.

- Millennials are the generation raised on values of self-esteem, specialness, and to "be oneself."

There is a direct relationship between the weakening of large institutions and the strengthening of individualism.

- Authority has shifted away from the official to the nonofficial for centuries.

Individualism is a generally positive development.

- Individualism is the embodiment of the Enlightenment ideal of self-autonomy.

Excessive individualism is encouraging an attitude of "it's all about me."

- "Me first" culture is a breeding ground for selfishness, egotism, and narcissism.

The rising tide of individualism is both a challenge and an opportunity for organizations.

- Creating personal relationships is more difficult but leads to higher rewards if successful.

Opportunities
Cater to ascending individualism.

- People are claiming their inalienable right to think and act on their own.

(continued)

Future Trend 1 (*continued*)

Present your product or service as a vehicle of individualism.

- A thing or experience that furthers the sense of being unique.

Wrap your organization or brands around the supreme power of the self.

- People everywhere are finally triumphing over the historical hegemony of church and state.

Use large, bureaucratic institutions as a foil to endorse the ethos of individualism.

- Apple's "1984" commercial is still the best expression of antiauthoritarianism and self-determination.

Draw upon the universal desire for each of us to realize our full potential.

- "Be all that you can be."

Offer bespoke opportunities for consumers.

- Personalize or customize your organization's deliverables.

Future Trend 2: Secularization

"The latest research on worldwide trends shows that religious beliefs are deteriorating," reports onenewsnow.com, adding that at the same time "those adhering to a secular belief system devoid of God are on the rise."[5] Various recent studies have also shown that secularism—literally the separation of religion from government—is proliferating, a function of the decline of both church and state. Churches all over the world are shutting down as more people lose their religion and, in its place, acquire a moral compass grounded in humanist values. (Humanism is a philosophy that does not incorporate a divine entity or supernatural beliefs, and assigns people the responsibility of living ethical lives.)[6] Atheism and agnosticism are thus growing, so much so that in some countries (notably Great Britain and Norway), there are more nonbelievers than believers.[7]

Even in the United States, a profoundly religious nation, more citizens are adopting secular humanism as their creed of choice. About 80 percent of Americans have consistently claimed to be members of a particular religion, but that figure is gradually dropping due to a generational effect.[8] Baby boomers have turned out to be significantly less religious (but more spiritual) than their "greatest generation" parents, and millennials are showing signs of continuing this pattern. As older churchgoers die off, houses of worship are having trouble filling their seats, with no great awakening on the horizon to reverse the drift. In fact, it's now atheists and agnostics who are increasingly banding together either online or at Meetups to share their beliefs (or lack thereof) with like-minded people. Growing up in a predominantly Christian community may have been tough for the nonreligious, but that is fast changing in America and elsewhere.[9]

While in some areas of the world such as sub-Saharan Africa, religion (Christianity, to be specific) is gaining ground, that is more the exception than the rule. With its population of 1.4 billion, China is highly secular, a function of the Communist government's successful efforts to steer people away from religion. Secularization is also rising in nations with official state religions because of anti-government sentiment. In the West, Islamophobia appears to be fueling what has been termed the New Atheism, as many come to see religion as a whole as more of a problem than anything else. Both financial security and education are tied to secularization, making it not surprising that religion is on the wane in developing nations with a growing middle class. The increase of women in the workplace and of households with fewer children also correlate with a decline in religious values, and the aging of the global population is likely another contributing factor. The Internet too is promoting secularization by exposing people to alternative forms of spirituality and by allowing nonbelievers to connect.[10]

Despite the growing numbers of Muslims in the world (Pew Research estimates that their numbers will increase from roughly 23 percent of the global population in 2010 to around 30 percent in 2050), it's difficult to make the case that fundamental religion will play a greater role in most of our lives in the future.[11] Ever since the Renaissance, in fact, the philosophy of secular humanism has spread throughout much of the world, along with a growing faith in the promise of science versus religion.[12] ("Science and religion are incompatible because they have different methods for getting knowledge about reality," Jerry A. Coyne wrote is his 2015 book *Faith Versus Fact*.)[13] A long view suggests that official forms of religion are, as the saying goes, "on the wrong side of history," and that humanism will seed further secularization in the twenty-first century.

Future Trend 2: Secularization

Decision-Making and Leadership Platform

Implications

Religion has been on the wane for the last half-millennium.

- The world as a whole is becoming more secular.

Science and technology are trumping the supernatural.

- The tangible and useful > the magical and mystical.

Humanist values grounded in taking responsibility for one's own actions are displacing belief in a supreme being.

- Reliance is on a personally defined set of ethics for the real world versus a leap of faith in the unknown.

Pockets of religious intensity are being countered by a broader sweep of secularization.

- It is the function of an array of key economic, social, and political factors.

Secularization is related to the larger rejection of institutional authority.

- It is another expression of individualism and autonomy.

Predicted jihad between Muslims and non-Muslim world is unlikely.

- Religion overall is becoming less relevant.

Opportunities

Embed humanistic values within your organization's charter.

- It's difficult to argue against people making a personal commitment to live ethical lives.

Celebrate secularization as a liberating force in people's lives.

- Freedom of faith is a relatively new thing in much of the world.

Trade upon what secularism is much about: antiauthoritarianism.

- Encourage resistance against official forms of power and control.

(*continued*)

Future Trend 2 (*continued*)

Present top-down, institutional forms of hegemony as contrary and antithetical to humanism.

- It is a common enemy that can bring people of all backgrounds closer together.

Appeal to millennials' attraction to secularism.

- The generation is growing up in an era of rapid decline of both church and state.

Stick to the facts in corporate communications and messaging.

- More trust is in what is known versus unknown.

Future Trend 3: Acceleration

Noticed that time seems to be constantly speeding up? You're not alone. Ever-evolving technology has a lot to do with the feeling that life is getting faster and faster, of course, as every few years a new device appears that allows us to do something more quickly and efficiently. More and more real-time services, live-streamed entertainment, and 24/7 access also provide the sense that there are fewer hours in any given day than there used to be even though no one has tinkered with our clocks or calendars. The faster adoption rate of new technologies is another major factor for the impression that time is accelerating. It took decades for most people to own telephones and radios but hundreds of millions of users signed onto Facebook in just a few years, and there is no reason to think that this phenomenon will reverse in the future. "As fast as innovation has multiplied and spread in recent years," McKinsey & Company advised, "it is poised to change and grow at an exponential speed beyond the power of human intuition to anticipate."[14]

While technological innovation is its main engine, acceleration—an increase in speed and, specifically, in the rate of progress—can be detected easily in other areas of everyday life. Time is money, as Ben Franklin famously wrote, a proverb that appears to be truer than ever with regard to how we work. Politics has become a revolving door and popularity contest compared to the eras of the past, and many if not most cities in the world are in a constant state of renewal. Most tellingly, perhaps, the speed in which we acquire and dispose of things—the cycle of consumerism—has increased, a function of the Next Big Thing continually coming around the corner.[15]

People who specialize in such things argue that acceleration is more than just a nagging feeling that life is speeding by. The impressive-sounding International Geosphere-Biosphere Programme (IGBP), an organization that studied global change, found in its research that the "human enterprise" did indeed experience "dramatic acceleration" along social, economic, and environmental lines over the past two centuries. Things really picked up in the 1950s, according to the IGBP, with some even making the case that the earth entered a new epoch in that decade. Production and consumption, as well as their environmental impact, rapidly escalated during what the organization called the "Great Acceleration," a period of time in which we are still living.[16]

For accelerationists, however, the already dizzying pace of the world is not enough. Once an outlying philosophy that sprang out of countercultural science fiction, accelerationism posits that both technology and global capitalism should be sped up as much as possible in order to advance mankind. A growing movement, accelerationism is consistent with a number of Future Trends (automation, transhumanism, deregulation, and anti-politics), and rests on the supposition that since change is inevitable it should be aggressively pursued. "Accelerationism, therefore, goes against conservatism, traditional socialism, social democracy, environmentalism, protectionism, populism, nationalism, localism and all the other ideologies that have sought to moderate or reverse the already hugely disruptive, seemingly runaway pace of change in the modern world," as Andy Beckett described it for the guardian.com.[17] In some ways an extreme version of Ayn Rand's objectivism, accelerationism presents technology-driven capitalism as the Manifest Destiny of the twenty-first century, and poses major implications for the future.

Future Trend 3: Acceleration

Decision-Making and Leadership Platform

Implications
The world is becoming effectively faster.

- There has been a quickening pace of life since the Industrial Revolution and especially since the postwar years.

Exponential technological innovation is driving acceleration in the Information Age.

- Digital devices are enabling us to do more things in less time.

(continued)

Future Trend 3 (*continued*)

Our "now" and "on demand" society is also making time seem more precious.

- There are greater expectations to have things and experiences instantly or ASAP.

Datedness and obsolescence are other contributing factors to the shrinking of time.

- The speedier introduction of new and improved products and services is shortening the consumption cycle.

Acceleration is tied to the expansion of laissez-faire capitalism and the decline of government.

- Free markets are allowing progress to go almost unchecked.

There is a range of psychological ills blamed on acceleration.

- These include anxiety, stress, sleeplessness, and cultural vertigo.

Opportunities
Speed up or be left behind.

- People want things now versus later.

Delight consumers by saving them time.

- Time is the most valuable form of currency.

Create products or services that will help those in a hurry to further speed up their lives.

- The ability to do more things in less time is the strongest selling point for accelerationists.

Package time in new and innovative ways.

- Provide services that allow customers to do what they would prefer to do.

(*continued*)

Future Trend 3 (*continued*)

Go against the acceleration grain by offering consumers ways to slow down.

- Life is a matter of quality versus quantity.

Disrupt acceleration via Future Trend 20 (Analogism).

- Offer non-digital things and experiences that provide a sense of stability in an unstable world.

Future Trend 4: Less-is-More

"Well, less is more, Lucrezia," went a line in Robert Browning's 1855 poem "Andrea del Sarto," and the rest, as they say, is history.[18] Architect and designer Ludwig Mies van der Rohe took the phrase and ran with it a century or so later, creating a new kind of modernist style predicated on simplicity and clarity.[19] Flash forward to the 1990s when a fair number of Americans, weary of the continual quest for "more" and "better," latched onto the rather radical idea that less could somehow be more. "Stress" had become a defining characteristic of the American Way of Life after the consumerist binge of the 1980s, causing some to wonder if all the cars, vacations, and dinners in fancy restaurants were worth what they cost in emotional terms. Life seemed to be mostly about "stuff" and to-do lists, these folks were concluding, making them, more than anything else, caretakers of things. In short, these people felt they had little or no control over their lives, and that some kind of change was in order. The movement was quickly labeled "voluntary simplicity," an acknowledgement that adherents were choosing austerity rather than having it thrust upon them.[20]

Today, less-is-more has evolved into a worldwide movement based in conscious minimalism that is tied to social and environmental responsibility. The economic kerfuffle of 2008 was instrumental in making people differentiate between their needs and wants, and helped to further the belief that a more restrained form of consumerism could actually be psychically liberating. Two other mega-forces—the green movement and what could perhaps be called "global sensibility"—also blossomed over the past decade, creating an ideal cultural climate for the philosophy of less-is-more to thrive.[21]

Less-is-more is also a response to a marketplace that has become literally overwhelming. The number and variety of choices in any given product category has become absurd, a result of companies trying to grab every little fraction of market share. (Check out Borat's cruising of a modern supermarket's cheese aisle in that titular film as prime—and hilarious—evidence of consumerism run amok.) In the process of market hyper-segmentation, however, companies have made things more difficult for the shopper, precisely the opposite of what they should be doing. Colgate, for example, lists forty-seven different kinds of toothpaste on its website (not including different sizes), and the typical supermarket in the United States stocks more than 42,000 items—almost five times the number in 1975.[22] In his 2004 *The Paradox of Choice*, psychologist Barry Schwartz convincingly showed how more could be less, and that it was in marketers' best interests to limit product selection.[23]

Happily, many marketers now appear to be responding to consumers' interest in simplifying their consumptive lives. "At a time when choices of all sorts are multiplying like weeds, simplicity is becoming a selling point, with more businesses trimming their product lines or otherwise making it easier to compare their wares," noted Neil Howe on forbes.com. It is not a coincidence that less-is-more marketing is becoming a go-to strategy just as millennials begin reaching their peak earning and spending years. Unlike baby boomers, for whom more was definitely more when they hit their stride as consumers during the Reagan era, millennials prefer a limited number of choices in everything as they seem to innately understand what Schwartz found in his research. "More than any other generation, millennials see scaled-back inventories as a way to make their lives easier," Howe added— refreshing news that organizations should heed.[24]

Future Trend 4: Less-is-More

Decision-Making and Leadership Platform

Implications
Less really can be more.

- There is much anecdotal evidence and hard research showing that consumerism in heavy doses can be overwhelming.

The preference for less is a broader-based, global version of voluntary simplicity.

- Less-is-more is being strengthened by social awareness and environmentalism.

(*continued*)

Future Trend 4 (*continued*)

The cultural shift from materialism to Experientialization (Future Trend 6) is also driving austerity.

- There is a greater recognition that doing is more rewarding than owning.

There is a backlash against out-of-control product proliferation in play.

- Consumers are leading marketers to limit the number of choices in any given category.

Millennials are the kings and queens of less-is-more.

- They possess a native intelligence that having fewer choices (and less stuff) is a good thing.

Less-is-more is becoming the new normal in the developed world.

- The growing middle class in emerging nations is still interested in acquisition.

Opportunities
Offer consumers less versus more.

- Streamline brand portfolios to win over those averse to over-the-top consumerism.

Borrow van der Rohe's approach to design in corporate imaging and communications.

- Deliver simplicity and clarity in tone and execution.

Present less-is-more as a highly evolved, socially aware, and morally just ethos to which to subscribe.

- Less-is-more is good for individuals and society as a whole.

Position yourself against competitors who promote a more-is-more philosophy.

- Excessiveness and extravagance are out of synch with the cultural and economic climate.

(*continued*)

Future Trend 4 (*continued*)

Define less-is-more as living the life one wants to lead without regard to status.

- Life is increasingly being seen as a journey versus a destination.

Turn the idea of upward mobility on its head in advertising.

- Feature "downwardly mobile" people who are happier than they used to be.

Future Trend 5: Experientialization

In their 1999 *The Experience Economy*, Joseph Pine and James Gilmore captured what would turn out to be the most compelling expression of consumer culture in the twenty-first century. The book, which is now considered a classic, argued that in order to get consumers' attention in an increasingly competitive climate, businesses had to experientialize their brands. Too many products and services were drifting into the netherworld of me-too commodities, the authors pointed out, making it vital that companies add value by shifting the focus away from the things themselves and toward the kinds of experiences they provided. The marketing model that had worked so well for so long—selling the particular features and benefits of a brand—had been displaced by one predicated on how a business could somehow enrich consumers' lives.[25]

Almost twenty years later, the experience economy has evolved into more of a way of life for many people around the world. "Just as materialism and the consumer revolution transformed standards of living in the 20th century," wrote the futurist James Wallman, "so I believe experientialism and an 'experience revolution' can transform quality of life in the 21st century." Owning things is giving way to doing things as a priority, one can safely say, a wholesale shift in the way people view the world and what they want to accomplish while they're alive. The rise of what I call experientialization has much to do with the diminishing returns of materialism (i.e., the dissatisfaction that comes with the never-ending quest to acquire possessions). As well, the green movement has ridden shotgun with experientalization as it became evident that the perpetual pursuit of stuff is not a sustainable proposition for individuals or society.[26]

Since the publication of *The Experience Economy*, numerous research studies have shown that materialism is not a particularly good path to realize happiness in one's life. In fact, the energy required to buy and take care of things is often a primary source of stress, raising the good question of why so many of us are heavily invested in an acquisition-based lifestyle.[27] The work-hard-so-I-can-play-hard paradigm is waning, however, replaced by a set of values that puts experience (versus making money) first. Not just the future of work but consumerism is tilting decidedly toward doing instead of owning. "The secret to happiness?" *Forbes* recently asked its readers, the answer being to "spend money on experiences, not things."[28]

Much attention has understandably been paid to millennials' prioritization of experience over materialism, especially their general apathy toward owning the big-ticket items of a home and car. Renting and traveling is a better use of limited funds, they sensibly demonstrate, particularly when so many of them are in debt up to their ears because of college loans.[29] Millennials "value living a life of purpose and direct their attention to discover meaningful experiences that build on their 'authentic self,'" explains Linda Tan, strategic insights director at ZenithOptimedia.[30] As well, the ways in which the members of that generation document their everyday goings-on on social media, particularly Instagram and Snapchat, provide firm evidence that life is essentially a series of experiences.[31] All generations use Facebook and other social media to provide friends and family with a kind of (carefully edited) narrative of their lives, however, and virtually all consumers are interested in adding to what can be called their "experiential portfolio." Money comes and goes but memories—the residue of experience—can last a lifetime, a philosophy to which more people will continue to subscribe.

Future Trend 5: Experientialization

Decision-Making and Leadership Platform

Implications
The desire for experiences is eclipsing that for things.

- Life is being defined increasingly in experiential versus acquisitional terms.

Experientialization represents a paradigmatic shift in consumer culture.

- Quality of life is more about what one does than what one owns.

(continued)

Future Trend 5 (*continued*)

Materialism is on the wrong side of the proactive pursuit of happiness.

- It is a brief bump of elation instead of long-term contentment.

Environmental concerns are another contributing factor for experientialization.

- Considerable resources are required for the endless cycle of production and disposal.

Deeper existential forces are also at work.

- There is a rising ethos of carpe diem, especially within youth culture.

Pay-as-you-go form of consumerism is gaining popularity in an increasing number of product and service categories.

- The debt associated with the ownership of expensive items is seen as a burden.

Opportunities

Experientialize your brands.

- Consumers are interested in spending money on doing versus owning.

Consider how your product or service can contribute to consumers' "experiential portfolio."

- Assets are increasingly viewed in active versus possessive terms.

Present experientialization as a sustainable proposition to younger people.

- Fun is not a diminishing resource.

Define your organization as an agent of happiness.

- Dedicate it to making the lives of people more pleasurable and joyful in some way.

Help consumers discover their "authentic selves."

- What kind of meaningful experiences can your company offer to facilitate this process?

Perceive your business as a marketer of not just experiences but memories.

- Consciousness is a collection of what one can remember.

Future Trend 6: Androgyny

It all started with Coco Chanel. The French fashion designer began to make clothing about a hundred years ago, with the first women's pantsuit part of her more gender-neutral aesthetic. Many women were ecstatic to be liberated from the layers of Victorian attire, a fashion counterpart to the suffragette movement that was bubbling up at the same time.[32] A half-century after this early example of gender blurring, unisex clothing became briefly fashionable, part of the turn-everything-upside-down ambitions of the counterculture. That laid the seeds for the androgynous style of the 1970s most conspicuously presented by "drag rock" artists like David Bowie and Queen.[33]

Now, almost another half-century after the world was introduced to the likes of Ziggy Stardust, androgyny is reaching a new level of popularity. "The idea that gender is a social construct is being explored in the fashion world this season," reported Molly Hannelly of moodfabrics.com in 2017, noting that "designers are finding ways to push gender identity in new and exciting ways."[34] Collections by a handful of the best-known designers included dresses worn by male models, making critics wonder if we were entering a new era in not just unisex clothing but unisex in general. Some young men belonging to Generation Z—people born around the turn of the twenty-first century—have taken to wearing makeup, another sign of the breakdown in traditional gender norms.[35] And some experts are making a case for "androgynous conscious" in the raising of children, thinking that prescribed gender roles are narrow and limiting. Girls should learn how to be assertive, linear, and authoritative, psychologist Shefali Tsabary argues, while boys should know how to be vulnerable and get in touch with their feelings.[36]

One might dismiss the prospect of a generation of sensitive young men in skirts and makeup as silly, but there is much more going on. As Hannelly suggested, the idea that gender is a social (versus purely biological) construct is gaining traction, in part a byproduct of the women's and gay rights movements as well as greater tolerance for "diversity" in general. As America and the world have become more multicultural over the past half-century or so, there has been a greater recognition that the buckets into which we sort people—gender, age, race, ethnicity, nationality, ability, sexual orientation, etc.—are more socially created divisions than anything else. One is who one is regardless of the age, color, or physical characteristics of our bodies, this idea goes, an interesting notion that is bound to become more accepted as machines begin to alter the definition of what makes someone human.

In a piece called "Gender Issues: Futures and Implications for Global Humanity," Ivana Milojevic captured the essence of why our future is likely to be a more androgynous one. We *act* as men or women because that is what society dictates we do, she explains, this a lot different from actually *being* men or women. "Humans engage in the cultural behaviours of practicing femininity and masculinity," Milojevic wrote, and "gender categories are much more fluid than simply those of women/men." It clearly appears that gender is a continuum versus being absolute, with most people possessing a blend of what we consider to be feminine and masculine traits. As gender becomes increasingly destabilized by science, technology, and further feminization (Future Trend 37), there will be greater acceptance to explore one's personal set of "male" and "female" characteristics or androgynous profile. For Milojevic, this will be a very good thing, resulting in "more democratic and fairer societies with flattened hierarchies."[37]

Future Trend 6: Androgyny

Decision-Making and Leadership Platform

Implications
The binary gender model is gradually becoming less rigid.

- Many people are increasingly receptive to the idea of a gender spectrum.

Holistic gender identity is seen by some as a more evolved form of human being.

- Exclusively "male" or "female" is narrow and limiting.

Androgyny is approaching mainstream.

- Youth culture is leading the way to a new concept of gender.

Greater fluidity in gender identity is the natural result of a new kind of approach to child raising.

- Conscious efforts are being made to avoid "boy" and "girl" stereotyping.

Gender neutrality is considered cool in popular culture.

- Creatives in the fashion and entertainment industries are serving as role models for hipper Generation Zers.

(continued)

Future Trend 6 (*continued*)

There is much more androgyny to come as the lines between man and machine get blurrier.

- The fusion of technology and human biology will make gender almost irrelevant.

Opportunities
Lean toward gender neutrality in corporate operations and communications.

- Defining people as masculine and feminine is increasingly out of favor.

Explore unisexual branding.

- Offer products and services that are not gender-defined.

Employ gender-neutral iconography when speaking to Generation Z and millennials.

- Demonstrate not just tolerance for but celebration of difference.

View consumers in other terms than socially defined constructs.

- Avoid bucket-sorting by gender, age, race, ethnicity, nationality, ability, sexual orientation, etc.

Anticipate much more gender blending as youth culture assumes positions of power.

- There will be greater ability to move up and down the male-female spectrum as one likes.

Prepare for a future multi-gender or gender-free world.

- Equip people with androgynous capabilities and permanently retire masculine/feminine dualism.

Future Trend 7: Pharmacopeia

For as long as there have been people, there have been drugs, and there is little reason to believe that will ever change. In fact, there is sufficient evidence to make the case that we are entering a new era in the consumption of drugs, one I call pharmacopeia. Social norms are colliding with scientific breakthroughs that will make the future a golden age for naturally and chemically induced altered states, I believe, with both legal and illegal forms of pharmacopeia to become mainstream.

For a glimpse of the future of drugs, there is no better source than VICE, the edgy media outlet that covers, in the editors' words, "everything that matters." With regard to our druggier future, Max Daly of VICE lists three certainties:

> Certainty #1: Until the planet explodes, melts, or drowns, humans will want to get intoxicated;
>
> Certainty #2: People who supply these intoxicants, particularly banned ones, will pocket a load of cash; and
>
> Certainty #3: We will be blindsided by a new drug phenomenon, a bolt from the blue, that everyone will pretend they knew was coming.[38]

As Future Trend 50 discusses, a wave of nootropics or smart drugs is coming our way as a means to help people do whatever they want to do better. Top scientists agree that within five or ten years, there will be a host of substances designed to enable users to "learn, think, relax, sleep, or simply to forget, a bit like the creepy, hangoverless pleasure drug Soma in Aldous Huxley's *Brave New World*," as Daly puts it.[39]

In addition to this category of "soft" drugs, pharmacopeia will consist of a group of harder mind benders, with much of it available for purchase online. (Like many staple businesses of the past, the local drug dealer is rapidly being disintermediated.) There is already a thriving "dark market" on the Internet in which a variety of drugs including MDMA, LSD, liquid mushrooms, and good old marijuana can be had. (Buyers and sellers communicate via the encryption messaging system Tor, with Bitcoin the payment method of choice.) The FBI, Europol, and various other law enforcement agencies shut down larger drug sites from time to time, but they soon pop up again under different names. In fact, more online drug sellers are moving their operations to the "clear" web and market their goods via a subscription model as a kind of Drug-of-the-Month Club. The online drug business is "tipping over from early adopters into the mainstream," notes Mike Power, author of *Drugs 2.0: The Web Revolution That's Changing How the World Gets High*, believing, "it will get bigger, easier to use, and more widespread."[40]

As marijuana becomes legal in more states, in part because of its proven medical benefits, harder psychedelics represent the next wave of drugs to become mainstream for both therapeutic and recreational use. Research has shown that MDMA can help ease the effects of PTSD among veterans, for example, and that psilocybin mushrooms can be of value to terminal cancer patients. Beyond a greater role in medicine, pharmacopeia will result from a greater recognition of the individual's right to do what one wants with his or her own mind. "It's a fundamental right to explore one's own consciousness," explained Rick Doblin, founder of the Multidisciplinary Association for Psychedelic Studies, seeing "freedom of thought" as just as essential as our other freedoms guaranteed by the Constitution.[41]

Future Trend 7: Pharmacopeia

Decision-Making and Leadership Platform

Implications

Drugs are a permanent feature of the human condition.

- This is reflective of the perpetual desire to alter one's consciousness.

Legal boundaries are not an effective barrier to the consumption of drugs.

- The right to how one thinks and perceives the world transcends official forms of authority.

Science will dramatically expand the range of drugs available.

- There will be more targeted purposes and emotional states from which to choose.

The selling and buying of drugs is shifting online.

- This reflects the classic efficiencies and limitless selection of e-commerce.

Medical use of drugs will help legitimize pharmacopeia.

- The lines between therapeutic and recreational use will get increasingly blurry.

Pharmacopeia will be combined with augmented and virtual reality technologies.

- The combination provides a powerful one-two punch of alternative realities or parallel universes in which to dwell.

(continued)

Future Trend 7 (*continued*)

Opportunities
Tap into the basic human wish to vary one's states of consciousness.

- This is a timeless and profitable business model.

Seize consumers' relentless desire to learn, think, relax, sleep, or simply to forget.

- We are still in the early stages of the science of the mind.

Celebrate individuals' fundamental right to freedom of thought.

- The body and mind are in one's own domain.

Uncover alternative therapies that can help people feel better.

- There is a continual, growing demand for anything promising to alleviate mental or physical distress.

Describe the deliverables of your product or service in terms of a different form of consciousness.

- There is an enduring interest among consumers to escape the ordinariness of reality.

Go to school on the marijuana revolution.

- The legalization of weed is just the tip of the pharmacopeia iceberg.

Future Trend 8: Easternism

In 1968, the Beatles went to India to take part in a Transcendental Meditation (TM) session at the ashram of Maharishi Mahesh Yogi. Led by George Harrison, the Beatles' interest in TM not only changed Western attitudes about Indian spirituality but ushered in a wholesale fascination with Eastern ways. Twenty-something baby boomers were most intrigued by the East, part and parcel of their countercultural notion of rejecting their parents' generation's way of life based in Western-style competition, conformity, and consumer capitalism. Buddhist philosophy meshed nicely with students' peace protests against the Vietnam War, and achieving a state of bliss through

TM and yoga (and psychedelics) became common among the American and European youth culture.[42]

A half-century later, George Harrison's sitar is still ringing in Westerners' ears. Eastern spiritualities have become mainstream, with many finding Buddhism to be an ideal alternative or complement to traditional Judeo-Christian religion. With their early exposure to Eastern philosophies, boomers continue to embrace Buddhism, and millennials too are shopping at what has been called "the spiritual marketplace." "Meditation, dharma teachers, retreat centers and monasteries, as well as some core terms (dharma, karma, mindfulness, zazen, bodhisattva, and metta, to name a few) have become well known and understood," observes writer and teacher Lewis Richmond. Westerners are also embracing Eastern healthcare practices *en masse*, with consumers of all stripes cruising the aisles of CVS, Walgreen's, and Duane Reed for natural remedies. Massage, acupuncture, herbal supplements, liquid vitamins, and essential oils are all part of this pursuit to stay healthy without resorting to drugs (and doctors).[43]

Acupuncture—the Chinese practice of stimulating certain areas of the body, usually by putting narrow needles into the skin—is growing especially fast as a form of alternative medicine. Acupuncture can help those with certain conditions avoid surgery, and research from a study at the National Institutes of Health has shown that the technique is effective in reducing chronic pain. By literally pinpointing a half-dozen energy points in the human body, acupuncture is said to reduce fatigue and help people stay active longer. Acupuncture is part of what some refer to as Traditional Chinese Medicine (TCM), which is expected to thrive in the years ahead. While Western science has yet to definitively prove that acupuncture has clinical efficacy, there is sufficient anecdotal evidence to suggest that it and other TCM modalities work. Unlike Western medicine, where a single doctor visit yields a prescription or referral, TCM works over time. The acceptance of Chinese medicine has been growing to the point where some insurance providers will cover treatments—some very good news indeed.[44]

More Americans and Europeans are also opting for Eastern fitness regimens such as qigong that offer an alternative to extended cardiovascular workouts designed to build strength. The aim of qigong is to bring about "qi" (spoken as "chee"), the Chinese concept of curative energy that moves like a current throughout one's body. Participants follow a teacher engaged in deep-breathing exercises combined with a set of flowing motions involving various parts of the body, especially the joint areas. The soaring interest in Eastern exercise practices like qigong is a function of Westerners' desire to achieve wellness via a more integrated mind-body-spirit philosophy. Health clubs are sensibly responding by filling classes with kinder and gentler activities imported from Asia, a sign of bigger things to come as more Eastern modalities roll West.[45]

Future Trend 8: Easternism

Decision-Making and Leadership Platform

Implications

The West is becoming more Eastern as the East becomes more Western.

- Omniculturalism (Future Trend 31) is at work.

Eastern ways are appealing to multiple generations.

- This is a function of boomer counterculturalism and millennial globalism.

The most compelling feature of Easternism is its holistic orientation.

- Americans and Europeans are increasingly keen on integrating mind, body, and spirit.

Another key aspect of Easternism is its spiritual foundation.

- It offers an attractive alternative to bipolar, judgmental Judeo-Christianity.

Consumers, physicians, and insurance companies are more receptive to an Eastern approach to health care.

- A preventive orientation aimed at wellness is more culturally in synch than pill-based Western medicine.

Fitness too is looking East.

- Movement is better than pounding for aging bodies.

Opportunities

Look East to help consumers maintain a sense of holistic wellness.

- Easternism is a meta-philosophy that can be applied to virtually all elements of an individual's lifestyle.

(continued)

Future Trend 8 (*continued*)

Adopt Easternism as an inclusive strategy.

- It cuts across social divisions of age, race, gender, ethnicity, nationality, etc.

Infuse your brands with a generous dose of Easternism.

- Swap rationalism, reasoning, logic, and linear thinking for the cosmic forces of yin and yang.

Launch brands that incorporate elements of mind-body-spirit.

- Introduce more evolved products and services for more evolved consumers.

Embed Eastern values in the deliverables of your product or service.

- Bring balance; focus; clarity; peacefulness; enlightenment; etc.

Bring some Zen to your organization.

- Offer workshops in meditation, yoga, Buddhism, mindfulness, qigong, tai chi, etc.

Future Trend 9: Wisdom

Fact: People who feel they are making strides up their personal evolution ladder are often not just healthy and happy but wise, or at least in the general vicinity. For centuries, the extremely wise have tried to decipher what constitutes wisdom, but there is still no consensus on exactly what it is, how it's acquired, and how it can be best put to use. Despite differing views on the subject, wisdom is usually seen as the result of a collection of experiences that culminates in the most advanced stage of life that a person can reach. The continual development (intellectually, socially, emotionally, and morally) needed to attain this ultimate phase of life implies that wisdom keeps building throughout one's years. Wisdom is believed to result in more fulfillment, gratification, and a sense of well-being, and can be beneficial to others and society at large. For all of these very good reasons, many people are striving for wisdom, a clear sign that it will represent a major pursuit in the future.[46]

The value of wisdom is not going unnoticed by researchers. One institution in particular—the University of Chicago's Center for Practical Wisdom—is leading the way in learning more about wisdom and seeing how it can be applied in real, everyday situations. Long ago, wisdom was considered a topic limited to arduous academic investigation in the noble pursuit of comprehending its makeup and value, making the center a throwback of sorts to the musings of the best and brightest of the ancients and the Renaissance. It is indeed hard to conceive a topic that can better indicate what humans are capable of, with the center's leadership perceiving that a fuller exploration of wisdom promises to spark new ideas regarding how our species can flourish.[47]

The Center for Practical Wisdom serves as a beacon of the future because it understands the critical role that wisdom can play in society. The mission of the center is to "deepen the scientific understanding of wisdom and its role in the decisions and choices that affect everyday life," an admittedly ambitious undertaking. "We want to understand how an individual develops wisdom and the circumstances and situations in which people are most likely to make wise decisions," these modern-day Socratae declare, "hoping that, by deepening our scientific understanding of wisdom, we will also begin to understand how to gain, reinforce, and apply wisdom and, in turn, become wiser as a society." Specific questions the center's researchers are asking are "What is the relationship between expertise and wisdom?"; "How does experience increase wisdom?"; and "What is the relationship between cognitive, social and emotional processes in mediating wisdom?"[48]

Rather than simply ponder such big questions of life, the Center for Practical Wisdom is putting its money where its mouth is. The center is connecting scientists, scholars, educators, and students at the university with researchers and scholars internationally who are interested in studying and understanding wisdom, and is leading the way in knowing more about the dynamics of wisdom, commissioning fresh research in the area, and publishing key discoveries. The center is also working to increase public interest in wisdom, raising the level of personal wisdom, and promoting the idea that our institutions could become wiser. "It is difficult to imagine a subject more central to the highest aspirations of being human," the center correctly states, adding that "the study of wisdom holds great promise for shedding light on and opening up new insights for human flourishing."[49] Wise words indeed as we look to a hopefully wiser future.

Future Trend 9: Wisdom

Decision-Making and Leadership Platform

Implications

Wisdom has been a desired destination for millennia.

- It is considered the most advanced stage of human development.

The cultural currency of wisdom is on the rise.

- Wisdom is something that must be earned rather than bought.

The aging of the global population is directly tied to the greater interest in wisdom.

- Wisdom is usually a function of experience.

There is more attention being paid to wisdom as its value is increasingly recognized.

- Wisdom is emerging as a legitimate field of study.

Finding solutions to our many social, economic, and political challenges demands more wisdom.

- Wisdom will be considered requisite for future generations of leaders as scientific research makes it more of a measurable trait.

Advances in neuroscience will possibly turn wisdom into a cognitive commodity.

- It would be a function of rewiring like other processes of the brain.

Opportunities

Offer consumers opportunities to raise their personal level of wisdom.

- Wisdom is a status symbol that is difficult or impossible to match.

Present your brands as agents of wisdom.

- Offer products or services that can allow individuals to be wiser in some way.

(*continued*)

Future Trend 9 (*continued*)

Commit to making your organization a voice of wisdom.

- Become a thought leader with a strong sense of social responsibility.

Partner with or lend some kind of support to the University of Chicago's Center for Practical Wisdom.

- Advance the cause of wisdom for the greater good of society.

Commission wisdom-related research specific to your industry.

- How can your business and your employees become wiser?

Name a Chief Wisdom Officer in your company.

- This person is responsible for ensuring that wisdom is a part of the decision-making process.

Future Trend 10: Self-Actualization

You remember the chart from a college psychology class. In his pyramid-shaped Hierarchy of Needs, Abraham Maslow proposed that there are five stages of life that people confront as they age. People are motivated to achieve certain needs, he wrote way back in 1943, the most basic one being physical survival. One must satisfy a lower need before progressing to a higher need, with our orientation to life and much of our behavior dedicated to climbing the next step. The first stage was biological and physiological needs (i.e., air, food, drink, shelter, warmth, sex, sleep); the second was safety needs (i.e., protection from elements, security, order, law, stability, freedom from fear); the third was love and belongingness needs (i.e., friendship, intimacy, trust and acceptance, receiving and giving affection and love, affiliating, being part of a group); the fourth was esteem needs (i.e., achievement, mastery, independence, status, dominance, prestige, self-respect, respect from others); and the fifth and final stage was self-actualization (i.e., realizing personal potential, self-fulfillment, seeking individual growth and peak experiences).[50]

While Maslow argued that just one out of a hundred people make it to the fifth, ultimate stage, he died almost a half-century ago. The affluent society of the past few decades has enabled many people to march up the pyramid toward self-actualization—a remarkable thing assuming of course that one believes the motivational theory of psychology has merit in real life. The self-help movement and development of a heavily therapeutic culture have also helped to push individuals up the pyramid; these are other major social forces that Maslow or anyone else could not have predicted when he published his original landmark paper during World War II.[51]

Today, self-actualization has emerged as a common goal among the more psychologically secure, and it is something that will become even more prevalent as the population ages and as the basic needs of millions or even billions of additional people are met. Although people are more likely to use terms such as "well-being" and "betterment" than "self-actualization," the idea is basically the same. (For the man who coined the term, self-actualization was the desire for fulfillment or, in his own words, "to become everything that one is capable of becoming.") As trendwatching.com has noted, individuals are actively trying to achieve their idealized identity as part of their endless quest for self-improvement and realization of their "authentic selves." Much of contemporary consumerism is really about self-actualization, one can argue, with brand choices made based on their relative ability to enable people to climb Maslow's ladder. "Consumers have moved beyond products as status symbols, and even moved beyond the 'experience' economy, to a place where self-actualization is the new status symbol," the smart folks at Trendwatching suggest.[52]

In fact, the path leading toward self-actualization through well-being in all dimensions of life is an idea that presents major opportunities for organizations of all kinds. Fostering a holistic, 360-degree sense of wellness and helping to provide a deep, emotional relationship between people and things and experiences are now how companies might consider defining their vision and mission. As well, much as with wisdom, more self-actualized people can help create a better world, making it a noble pursuit on all levels. "Self-actualization is the new carrot everyone is chasing," Melissa Thompson wrote in newsblaze.com in 2016, thinking that "the potential for people to self-actualize is higher than it has ever been before."[53]

Future Trend 10: Self-Actualization

Decision-Making and Leadership Platform

Implications
Individuals are consciously or unconsciously evolving.

- People (hopefully) climb through Maslow's hierarchy of needs as they mature.

(continued)

Future Trend 10 (*continued*)

The highest level of the hierarchy is a goal that transcends wealth or power.

- Realizing one's full potential is the ultimate achievement for any human being.

More people are pursuing self-actualization due to major social and economic factors.

- Middle-classing (Future Trend 15) and Graying (Future Trend 35) are creating an ideal cultural climate for personal growth.

The focus on the self is also helping people climb the ladder.

- Individualism (Future Trend 1) is the basis for fulfilling one's own needs.

Other cultural forces are also in play

- Easternism (Future Trend 8) and Wisdom (Future Trend 9) are much about the evolution of the self.

Being all that you can be is a new and laudable form of status.

- Self-actualization is good for individuals and society at large.

Opportunities

Define your brand as an opportunity for consumers to achieve self-actualization.

- The realization of one's full potential is far beyond the usual reason-for-being for any product or service.

Foster a holistic, 360-degree sense of well-being or "betterment."

- Nurturing a deep relationship between people and things and experiences is an advanced form of marketing.

Dangle the carrot of self-actualization before individuals.

- Self-actualization is a tantalizing incentive for a growing number of people to try reaching.

(*continued*)

Future Trend 10 (*continued*)

Trade on our entrenched therapeutic culture.

- Many are already engaged in a process of self-improvement, personal growth, and the pursuit of happiness.

Pay particular attention to baby boomers.

- Achieving one's idealized identity is often a primary objective in the third act of life.

Strive for your organization to become self-actualized.

- How can your company realize its full potential?

CHAPTER TWO

~

Economic Trends

Hope you're prepared for the economic free-for-all that looms in our collective future. Laissez-faire—the economic system in which governments refrain from interfering with the workings of the marketplace—is increasingly the order of the day, part of the global shift toward populism and anti-bureaucracy. As free market capitalism sweeps through all corners of the world, a lingering function of the breakdown of the Soviet Union and its communist outposts, a philosophy of may-the-best-man-or-woman-win is guiding economic thought and practice. The result is a strange brew of polarization and concentration, with a growing middle class in some countries but greater economic division overall. The trend toward personalization and the emergence of microbrands suggest that decision makers must be able to focus, while trends such as deregulation and disintermediation make it clear that they also must have a good view of the big picture as well. The winners will thus be those who are best equipped to see the forest without losing sight of the trees.

Perhaps the best news for businesspeople is that a second great wave of consumerism is sweeping across much of the world, a wild pursuit for the good things in life that some experts believe is doing nothing less than "saving" the global economy from a deep recession or worse. A postindustrial economic climate in much of the West is not a good formula for growth, after all, with many of us not interested in significantly adding to the pile of stuff we already have. Running parallel with this simmering global economic gumbo is, of course, the seeping of digital technology into all nooks and crannies of everyday life. If there is one central theme of our economic future, it is the fact that we are increasingly connected globally, something that

41

poses major implications for any organization. The emergence of the online universe has effectively turned all of us into a single market of producers and consumers, a contemporary version of the trend toward globalization that has been evolving for centuries if not millennia. ("Global market integration is almost as old as humanity," the *Economist* noted in a fascinating article from 2013.)[1] Money itself is rapidly becoming digital, the ultimate sign perhaps that we have all become players on the global economic stage. The reinvention of the workplace from a rather neat and tidy model defined by both time (forty hours a week, generally) and space (an office of some kind) to one consisting largely of freelancers working anytime and anywhere is further turning the economy as we know it into something much different.

The overarching goal for most organizations and individuals keen on being actors on this stage is thus finding innovative ways to be more of a star than an understudy. The challenges to achieving success, however defined, are arguably greater than ever, and will be even more so in the future. Open markets and theoretically equal access to technology in a shrinking world mean a more intense competitive environment, for one thing, making the need to stand out in some way from the crowd (now numbering almost eight billion people) virtually imperative. The more we have in common as global citizens, the more we want to express our individuality, however, just one of many seeming contradictions informing the ten Future Trends in this chapter.

Given the ways in which the economic winds are blowing, organizations might first ask themselves how they can help people carve out their respective unique identities. It is this basic human desire to make our presence known that presents the biggest business opportunities, I believe, with good decision making and leadership revolving around the packaging of an organization's assets into products or services that individual consumers find meaningful and valuable. All signs are that the economic landscape of the future will be significantly more undefined, more reason for businesses of every sort to consider such thinking in both their short-range and long-range plans.

Future Trend 11: Deregulation

I have seen the future of economics and, regrettably, it is deregulation. Deregulation—the reduction or elimination of restrictions within a particular industry by the government in order to encourage business—is on the rise as a more laissez-faire economic climate sweeps over much of the world.[2] Populist leaders seeking election or politicians in office catering to corporate interests are repealing many laws passed during the heady days when consumer protection was considered a priority. Increasingly, there is the sentiment that an informed consumer is a good consumer, and the government should not be in the business of, well, business. Globalism is helping to fuel deregulation, as nations do not want to be at a competitive disadvantage by limiting what companies in those countries can and cannot do. "The market knows best" is becoming a mantra of the times, a philosophy that will guide economic policy for the foreseeable future.

So is deregulation good or bad? As with most controversial issues, it's a little of both. On the positive side, deregulation enables smaller players within an industry to be more innovative, allowing them to better compete with the big guys (and providing consumers with more inventive and interesting products). Deregulation also tends to lower prices, as market forces, versus regulatory agencies, determine what a product should cost the consumer. Most important, deregulation discourages the creation of monopolies, which often result as large corporations collaborate with those agencies to make the rules. On the negative end, deregulation often creates a more volatile economic environment characterized by booms and busts, and discourages the formation of new industries that require large initial start-up costs. As well, consumers are far more likely to experience inferior or dangerous products in a highly deregulated environment, or get burned by scams and frauds. Most serious, social responsibility tends to go out the window when regulation of a given industry disappears, with the environment in particular at great risk as companies prioritize profits over preservation of our natural resources.[3]

History vividly demonstrates the potential dangers of an industry that deregulates and the reactionary steps that often follow. Many experts, especially those in foreign countries, believe the deregulation of the American banking system in 1999 led to the global financial meltdown in 2008 when big banks bought bundles of high-risk subprime mortgages in order to improve their bottom lines. Deregulation of the energy industry by various states in the 1990s ultimately led to the Enron fiasco, and deregulation of the airline biz in 1978 effectively created today's oligopoly and its up-charging, underserving of less-trafficked markets, and turning of what was once a wonderful experience into a horrible one.[4]

These lessons of history clearly demonstrate that accelerating global competition and the pressure for short-term profits by shareholders are a perfect formula to drive corporations to place greed over ethics at the consumer's expense. Deregulation is unfortunately on the rise, however, as nations themselves cut costs and elect leaders who do not want to be seen as anti-business. How should organizations act in a more deregulated environment of the future? Taking full advantage of laissez-faire markets is all well and good, but there are strong plusses to be had by going against the deregulation grain. In short, companies should consider their own set of self-imposed regulations in order to best serve both consumers and their brands.

Future Trend 11: Deregulation

Decision-Making and Leadership Platform

Implications
Expect greater deregulation in your industry.

- The winds are shifting decidedly toward allowing the market to regulate itself.

More freedom to run a business without government interference is a likely scenario.

- There will be fewer restrictions and less bureaucratic red tape.

Deregulation is a definite plus for niche marketers.

- It is easier to find a competitive advantage without curbs and checks.

Larger players will benefit most from deregulation through a greater ability to lower prices.

- An increase in revenues is usually the result as products and services become more affordable to more people.

Deregulation is likely to lead to greater instability within an industry and in the economy as a whole.

- Fewer controls and constraints = more uncertainty and variability.

An influx of unscrupulous players is likely with little or no policing of industry.

- Greater deregulation is bad for both ethical businesses and consumers.

Opportunities
Stand out from the deregulated crowd by nurturing an image of an industry good guy.

- Take the high road by featuring in communications a strong sense of ethics grounded in principles of corporate responsibility.

Strictly enforce internal company guidelines to deter employees from engaging in dodgy activities.

- There is a greater ability to take shortcuts and hide information in a deregulated environment.

(continued)

Future Trend 11 (*continued*)

Take a leadership role in your industry by coauthoring quality standards.

- Encourage employees to be active members in relevant national associations.

Be a loud voice for consumer protection.

- Protect your industry from a bad reputation caused by dishonest competitors.

Partner with nonprofits that are highly trusted by consumers to maintain a positive image.

- These include the YMCA, United Way, American Red Cross, American Cancer Society, etc.

Make a special effort to serve underserved markets.

- Less affluent or trafficked areas are largely ignored because of lower margins.

Future Trend 12: Polarization

"This is almost certainly the highest level of relative, and certainly absolute, global inequality at any point in human history," observed the Institute for New Economic Thinking (INET) in 2015, wondering if there was "anything we can do to reverse or mitigate this trend." The INET reached that conclusion after talking with Branko Milanovic, a visiting presidential professor at the City University of New York. Milanovic sat down with Marshall Auerback of the INET in November of that year for a rather remarkable twenty-minute interview that serves as an excellent overview of the past, present, and future of global income inequality. Many if not most of the haves and have-nots continue to go in opposite directions, noted Milanovic, who is also affiliated with the World Bank and the Luxembourg Income Study Center, with the trend likely to continue through the twenty-first century unless some drastic steps are taken.[5]

What separates Milanovic from the rest of the economics pack is his global orientation and greater understanding that all nations and all citizens are indelibly connected with regard to how income and wealth are distributed. Most economists view the gap between the rich and the poor within specific countries, a helpful but narrow way to perceive the divide. When viewed internationally, however, that divide becomes significantly greater, making it easier to fully understand how uneven the slices of our global pie of money are. The wealthiest 5 percent of people around the world account for a full third of total income, Milanovic's research shows, a figure that is equal to the poorest 80 percent. From that perspective, just 15 percent of people on the planet can be considered middle class, a disturbing fact that proves how polarized the world really is in terms of economics. Much is being made about the growing middle classes in some Asian and South American countries, but the hard truth is that the disparity between the rich and poor in most of the world remains vast and appears to be getting bigger.[6]

With their focus on global income and wealth inequality, Milanovic, along with a few other scholars, has brought what was until quite recently an underground topic to light. Discussion around economic polarization was un-til a decade or so ago limited to the plight of developing nations, but that all changed with the 2008 financial fiasco. It was generally assumed that people of poorer countries were catching up along economic lines, but research done after that event showed that the rich bounced back quickly following the bursting of a bubble and then were able to significantly increase their wealth in a period of expansion. The top 1 percent make even the very rich look like paupers, we learned from the Occupy movement, with technological change and the gradual conversion from a manufacturing- to service-based economy major factors for the trend. In the United States, the minimum wage is quite a bit less than it was at its historic high in 1968 in real dollars, this too con-tributing to economic polarization.[7]

However far their respective scope of business extends, organizations have a moral (and likely financial) obligation to consider such immense economic inequality and, ideally, take steps to address it. Besides the obvious—poverty typically involves suffering—inequality is bad for business, dramatically re-ducing the number of people who can take part in the global marketplace. Expanding the middle class is good for individual nations and the world as a whole, making the flattening of the income and wealth curve something that more influential companies should try to include in their thought leadership platform and in long-term planning.

Future Trend 12: Polarization

Decision-Making and Leadership Platform

Implications

The global economic playing field is not at all an even one.

- A small fraction of people accounts for most of the money.

Growing middle classes in China and India are more the exception than the rule.

- They are not reflective of the world overall.

It is more accurate to view economics from a global perspective.

- A nation-by-nation analysis is fine but limiting.

It is incumbent upon any business to consider how vast global inequality relates to its mission and operations.

- Everyone and every organization are somehow players on the world stage.

The subject of economic inequality is likely to intensify in the future.

- There is a greater recognition that polarization is one of the biggest issues and problems of our time.

Enlarging the middle section of the global economic bell curve is in the best interests of all.

- More wealth in more people's hands is the best economic formula not just for business but for society as a whole.

Opportunities

Incorporate a global view of economics in your organizational charter.

- Polarities are affecting your business whether you know it or not.

Invest in local economies here and abroad.

- Real, measurable change is possible.

(*continued*)

Future Trend 12 (*continued*)

Consider adopting the middle-classing of the world as a cause.

- There is a growing attention to the situation, but its depth is not largely understood.

Partner with organizations dedicated to the plight of the poor.

- These include UNICEF, Doctors Without Borders, World Food Program USA, Feeding America, etc.

Host a forum on global economic inequality in order to further awareness of the issue.

- Live stream a discussion between economists with expertise in the area.

Pay employees more than the minimum wage.

- Study after study show that the minimum wage is at poverty level and is unable to support a family (and perhaps an individual).

Future Trend 13: Personalization

In her book *The Master Trend: How the Baby Boom Generation is Remaking America* published twenty-five years ago, Cheryl Russell astutely observed our recent shift from an industrial economy to a personalized one. "Customized goods, designed for individualistic consumers" was the basis for this new kind of economy, she noted in 1993, adding that "information about customers and their needs" was essential for marketers wishing to personalize their products and services. Russell cited cellular phones, video stores, and automated teller machines as good examples of the more personalized consumer landscape that was taking shape at the time, unaware that in just a couple of years the Internet would begin to revolutionize not only the economy but life as we knew it.[8]

Today, it is digital content that is most compellingly defining the personalized economy, with organizations interested in if not obsessed with what each of us gets to see on our individual screens. "The end game now is personalization," a white paper issued by *Forbes Insights* in 2016 stated, "an outcome that's constantly evolving as innovative companies find new ways to create meaningful experiences for each individual that fuse the online and offline worlds." Using gobs of data to create customized content is all the rage among more digitally engaged companies, according to Forbes, a hyper-version of Russell's advice for marketers to gather "information about customers and their needs." To get that done, Forbes lists five key practices—prioritizing goals, naming a "content champion," knowing customers through data, building capabilities, and measuring to optimize—a formula that may very well become the template for marketing in the future.[9]

Gartner Data & Analytics is another company pointing the way to the emerging personalized economy. "Companies are under significant pressure to leverage data," notes Lydia A. Clougherty Jones, an analyst for that company, seeing the juggling of digital information as ideally aligned with the Future Trend of personalization. Marketers in many industries such as health and wellness, banking, and retail are currently seizing the personalization day by offering consumers individualized products and services. "Consumers are flocking to innovative products that customize functionality to their personal preferences, and often to their unique physical and psychological characteristics," she continues, citing ingestibles, wearables, and embeddables as good examples of the application of advanced broadband technology and health care. Understandably, complying with privacy best practices is a major challenge for marketers going down this road.[10]

An even more extreme kind of personalized economy may loom in the future, however. "Increasingly, as individuals, we are consciously examining the economic systems into which we were born by default, and questioning their validity, utility, and reach," writes Melanie Swan in her FutureMemes blog, proposing that "the new sensibility could be that economic systems are determined at the level of the individual as opposed to the level of the nation-state." Swan and some others see personalized economic systems on the horizon, where each of us would have our own forms of currency, conversion mechanisms, and other features that would allow individuals to be the king or queen of his or her own mini-economy. A stretch, perhaps, but many of us have already built pretty complex social media platforms, making the notion of personalized economic platforms within the realm of possibility.[11]

Future Trend 13: Personalization

Decision-Making and Leadership Platform

Implications

The global economy is becoming increasingly personalized.

- We are shifting further away from a mass production/consumption model.

The online universe is ideally suited to accommodate personalization.

- "Personal computers" are inherently individualistic.

Digital content is taking personalization to an entirely new level.

- Data and analytics are the key to creating customized user experiences.

Privacy issues are running along a parallel path with personalization.

- Information gathering and sharing is now a fundamental part of being on the grid.

Individualized products and services are clearly the wave of the future.

- We may be approaching the day where everything consumed will be somehow unique.

The concept of personalized economic platforms is hard to imagine but feasible.

- Such platforms would be an extension of the breakdown of nation-states and the dissolution of large institutions.

Opportunities

Embed the concept of personalization in your company's deliverables.

- How can your organization best meet the needs and wants of individuals?

Use personalized medicine as a model for how to treat consumers as individuals.

- Health care is further along the curve of understanding that everybody (and every body) is different.

(continued)

Future Trend 13 (*continued*)

Create mash-ups of your brands as a personalization strategy.

- Cross-pollinations are a relatively easy way to multiply features and design elements.

Allow consumers to design individualized products and services.

- Create-your-own is the ultimate expression of personalization.

Measure the value of creating digital content and use of data and analytics before investing in them.

- Personal experiences in the real world are as good as or better than those online.

Make privacy of individuals a priority.

- Build data gathering into corporate ethics policy.

Future Trend 14: E-Currency

In November 2016, the Swedish bank Riksbank announced that it was considering introducing its own form of electronic (or e-) currency. This would be the first time a major bank issued e-currency, ushering in what might very well lead to a global shift toward virtual money. The use of cash is declining everywhere in the world but probably no more so than in Sweden, making that country a likely place for digital currency to become mainstream. Finding an ATM in Sweden is already like looking for a needle in a haystack, and a good number of retailers there no longer take cash.[12] E-currency, notably Bitcoin, works not unlike payment cards that let users make purchases anywhere and everywhere, a byproduct in part of the gradual move toward online shopping. While the various bugs of virtual money have yet to be ironed out, linking currencies to particular nations is an idea rooted in the past and one that has little or no place in the future.

Sweden may very well be an outlier, but it is not farfetched to believe that in the not-too-distant future banks in the United States and even the federal government will put e-currency into circulation. That is the prediction of Doug Casey, a "currency guru" with an impressive history of being right on the money, so to speak, on matters both economic and political. Casey thinks the US Federal Reserve will not just create its own form of digital currency but take steps to encourage people to use what he and others are calling "Fedcoin." Doing so would be a kind of a preemptive strike against all the foreign cryptocurrencies likely to emerge in the next decade or so; Fedcoin would initially be exchangeable with dollars and thus be a more stable form of virtual money.[13]

Much has been made about the cashless society, of course, yet paper and metal money remain heavily in circulation in most countries. A three-thousand-year habit is hard to break, after all, making it understandable why many of us are reluctant to give up cash completely. Watch how millennials pay for stuff, however, and you get a glimpse of how cash is becoming oh-so-twentieth-century. In fact, more than one-third of Americans and Europeans said they would be delighted to use e-currency versus cash if it were possible, according to a 2017 study completed by Ipsos for the ING bank website eZonomics, with at least 20 percent of those same people already doing exactly that despite the many obstacles. Nation-states with their own forms of currency are one of the bigger challenges facing the full blossoming of a cashless society, but geopolitical trends are strongly in favor of the advent of a borderless economy.[14]

One doesn't have to be a Nostradamus to realize that most of us will be using e-currency in our own respective lifetimes. Pointing and clicking versus rummaging through one's pants for that missing-in-action quarter is a lot more convenient, for starters, and it just makes sense that money becomes part of the ever-expanding online universe. It's important to remember that many of us were very nervous about paying for something online with a credit card through the late 1990s, and the fraud and money laundering that is still commonplace in the world of cryptocurrency is delaying the wholesale tossing of cash to the dustbin of history. Deregulation and globalization are each on the side of e-currency, however, suggesting that our economic future is going to look very different relatively soon. "It would be money without government regulation, recognized across the world, completely revolutionizing the way our global economy functions," correctly observed nuskool.com, something that I believe to be inevitable.[15]

Future Trend 14: E-Currency

Decision-Making and Leadership Platform

Implications
E-currency is on the way.

- Cash is gradually going extinct, especially among younger people.

Major banks will start issuing their own cryptocurrencies to gain a competitive advantage and protect their own interests.

- E-currencies will be seen as a means of retaining deposits and controlling assets.

The acceptance of e-currency in other nations will cause a trickle-up effect.

- International trade will act as a catalyst for digital money.

There are many problems to be resolved before e-currency eclipses cash in ordinary use.

- Criminal activity is always on the cutting edge of innovation.

E-currency is entirely consistent with technological, geopolitical, and social trends.

- Money is one of just a few arenas to remain heavily analog.

All kinds of other forces are in play as e-currency becomes the norm.

- There are major political and cultural implications should there be a universal (i.e., digital) form of currency.

Opportunities
Champion e-currency in your industry.

- Embrace the revolution that is currently taking place in the history of money.

Frame e-currency within the context of other global Future Trends.

- Digital currency is part of the bigger shift toward interconnectivity, automation, mobility, and living in 24/7 time.

(continued)

Future Trend 14 (*continued*)

Attract influential early adopters by expressing preference for e-payments.

- Offer incentives over traditional forms of payment (i.e., cash, check, and credit).

Partner with a major bank to help create an e-currency.

- A branded e-currency represents an opportunity for an organization to be part of the future of business.

Work with technology firms to create a proprietary form of e-currency.

- An industry-specific system offers competitive and/or consumer advantages.

Weave attention to security issues into all avenues of digital payment.

- Strive to be one step ahead of the bad guys.

Future Trend 15: Middle-Classing

So how can the world be economically polarizing yet middle-classing at the same time? Well, like many relationships described on Facebook, it's complicated. From a macro perspective, the world is indeed becoming increasingly divided along economic lines, but, in some countries with large populations, more people are entering the middle class. "Global middle-class growth will drive the world economy," predicts Homi Kharas, a senior fellow and deputy director of the Global Economy and Development Program at the Brookings Institution, seeing the trend as very good news for businesses large and small and for society overall. In his working paper for that organization published in 2017, Kharas argued that the global middle class was experiencing an "unprecedented expansion," one that he believed would continue for the foreseeable future. "The next decade could see a faster expansion of the middle class than at any other time in history," he gushed, with his research showing that in a few years "a majority of the world's population could have middle-class or rich lifestyles for the first time ever."[16]

For Kharas and other pro-capitalist types, the exciting thing about a growing global middle class is the prospect of billions of more consumers on the planet. Rather than use pure income levels as the primary measure of class, economists like Kharas choose spending or purchasing power as the most important indicator of one's socioeconomic status. Consumer spending in advanced economies is forecast to grow just .5 percent to 1 percent annually, while that of emerging economies could very well increase by 6 percent or greater yearly—very good news to businesses wishing to expand their markets. Most new members of the global middle class will want to fill up their homes with stuff, of course, and will be keen on buying autos, taking vacations, and attending entertainment and sports events, not to mention investing in healthcare, education, and financial services. China and India are the epicenters of middle-classing, with almost 90 percent of the next billion people who achieve that status in the near future likely to be Asian.[17]

While there will be 1.5 billion middle-class people in China and India in 2020, assuming that forecasts by the International Monetary Fund (IMF) prove accurate, citizens of other countries are also rapidly climbing the economic ladder. Brazil, Mexico, Pakistan, and Indonesia could very well have respective middle classes of more than one hundred million people in a few years, with Egypt, Nigeria, and Vietnam soon following. Economic status is also rising in the Philippines and Thailand, so much so that each of those countries could have a middle class as sizable as those in the United Kingdom, France, and Italy. Should one more billion people become middle class in the near future as predicted, more than four billion members will belong to the global middle class, making that group the largest portion of the world's population.[18]

Interestingly, Kharas argues that a burgeoning global middle class may actually help reduce rather than increase the earth's carbon footprint. While more consumption does indeed mean greater usage of natural resources, higher emission levels, and additional waste, middle-class women are much more likely to work outside the home than those who are poor. More women in the workforce means fewer babies, Kharas explains, with a significantly smaller global population more than counteracting the negative environmental consequences of greater consumption. "The emerging middle class should be viewed as a positive force for reduced carbon emissions, not as a contributor to faster climate change," he states, more reason we should hope that he's right.[19]

Future Trend 15: Middle-Classing

Decision-Making and Leadership Platform

Implications

A larger global middle class is good for everyone.

- Millions and possibly billions of people are escaping poverty.

It is odd but seemingly true that the global economy is polarizing yet also middle-classing.

- Richest of the rich and poorest of the poor are skewing the bell curve.

The international business community is exultant about a growing global middle class.

- Most industries and companies will benefit from more consumers with "average" purchasing power.

Asia is the undisputed world capital of the global middle class.

- Huge populations dwarf those of the West.

A global middle class is the ultimate triumph of consumer capitalism.

- A centuries-long process is finally reaching the four corners of the world.

The effect of a larger global middle class on the carbon footprint and climate change is much debated.

- More consumption is offset by lower population.

Opportunities

Gain a presence in nations that are middle-classing.

- These include China, India, Brazil, Mexico, Pakistan, Indonesia, Egypt, Nigeria, Vietnam, Philippines, Thailand.

Take lessons from the evolution of the middle class in advanced economies.

- History is repeating itself a century or so later.

Create brands that have the potential to cross over national and cultural boundaries.

- Strive to speak a lingua franca or Esperanto in marketing efforts.

(*continued*)

Future Trend 15 (*continued*)

Tap into those values common to a global middle class.

- These include aspiration, status-consciousness, etc.

Leverage the concept of "Americanness" in brand communications.

- The United States is a powerful symbol of middle-class and consumer culture.

Embed the ethos of corporate and social responsibility in global marketing plans and programs.

- Pay special attention to the environmental impact of consumerism.

Future Trend 16: Microbranding

"When you look at the ways society has changed over the past 50 years," writes Beth Novitsky, "it becomes clear that we have moved from a 'monolithic' culture—one in which everything was mass-produced from a single source on an industrial scale—to a 'mosaic' culture, where infinite choices, socioeconomic and racial diversity, globalization, and 24/7 on-demand access have broken brands into ever-smaller entities." Novitsky, a director at Gensler, an architectural and design firm, has a keen sense of the evolution of business during the last half-century, as well as how it is likely to progress in the future. Moving from an industry to a service economy and the fragmentation of the media universe have triggered the wholesale reinvention of the concept and practice of marketing, with the slicing and dicing effects of the Internet only compounding the process.[20]

The natural outcome of this historical arc of marketing is, not surprisingly, microbrands. Microbrands, according to Novitsky, offer "a clear point of view, targeted communication strategies, and opportunities for customization," correctly arguing that "megabrands that try to be all things to all people are relics of the past." More agile, resilient, and mutable than traditional brands, microbrands are more likely to survive and thrive in the more volatile economic and social climate that lies ahead. Like people and society as a whole, microbrands are able to evolve over time, making them entirely consistent with Darwinian theory grounded in adaptation. As well, the emergence of social communities scattered around the globe is an ideal framework in which to seed microbranding, something smart marketers are already doing.[21]

Indeed, success stories in microbranding are not difficult to find. Apple has been able to microbrand its individual products under an umbrella brand, and large department stores such as Nordstrom have had positive results from devoting space to popular niche brands such as customized shoe marketer Shoes of Prey. The microbranding of the beverage industry is probably the best example of this relatively new model of marketing. Microbrewers continue to nip at the heels of Anheuser-Busch and other megabrands, and Coca-Cola and Pepsico no longer dominate the beverage business as they used to. In fact, these companies have embraced the microbrand concept in a big way by introducing niche products that offer a closer relationship between marketer and consumer.[22]

If there is a single takeaway to be had from the flourishing of microbranding, it is that it reflects and exemplifies the rising value of nimbleness and dexterity. Through the twentieth century, size had served as an organization's (or nation's) most potent asset, with power to be realized through volume, mass, and sheer numbers. Now, however, contests are more likely to be won by the swift versus the biggest, with the ability to quickly change gears based on conditions another key asset to have in one's tool kit. As in geopolitics, engagement and sharing have replaced scope and scale in the world of business as important attributes to possess, pushing community building and storytelling to the forefront of a brand's reason for being. "It is these bespoke, artistically driven micro-brands that are the model of success for the future," observed Billee Howard, the founder of the creative consultancy Brandthropologie and author of *WE-Commerce: How to Create, Collaborate, and Succeed in the Sharing Economy*, envisioning a time when "the mantra won't be too big to fail, but too big to succeed."[23]

Future Trend 16: Microbranding

Decision-Making and Leadership Platform

Implications
The microization of brands is part of the larger cultural shift toward fragmentation and disintegration.

- This is related to the continual splintering of nation-states, institutions, and organizations.

Monolithic entities of all kinds are rapidly losing viability.

- A "multi-lithic" model is ruling the day in business and elsewhere.

(continued)

Future Trend 16 (*continued*)

Clarity, narrowness, and mutability are now primary brand assets.

- There is a greater need to have a distinct voice in the marketplace.

Community is at the heart of microbranding.

- Community = any size of group with some kind of shared interest.

Microbranding is in the relatively early stages of development.

- Large global brands still dominate in many industries due to decades of enjoying critical mass.

With exceptions, consumers are more likely to be attracted to highly defined brands.

- Ambiguity is a marketer's worst enemy.

Opportunities
Micro your brands.

- Offer consumers or constituencies a distinct, delineated set of deliverables.

Go after ignored market segments or niche audiences with a vengeance.

- Use precision targeting versus area carpeting.

Fight only those battles you have a chance to win.

- Concede market segments whose interests fall outside your core strengths.

Build resiliency and adaptability into your brands and corporate culture.

- Survival of the fittest is predicated on ability to adjust to (and ideally anticipate) change.

Identify communities of interest that align with microbrands' respective orbit.

- What values do a product or service share with the passions of a particular group of people?

Create brand stories as if they were characters in a novel or movie.

- What is the "heroic journey" of the product or service?

Future Trend 17: Fluidity

Like other mainstays of the twentieth century, the nine-to-five-based job in which workers sought long-term careers from employers (and vice versa) is fast becoming a memory. In its place is the freelance or "gig"-based economy, a reinterpretation of work that is reshaping business and the lives of millions of people across the world. Younger people in particular are attracted to this new version of work, less and less interested in adopting the rigid, single-employer model of their parents and grandparents. "The watchword of the new global economy is fluidity, thanks to the rise of freelance work," Faisal Hoque wrote for fastcompany.com, raising the possibility that our current definition of employment will be "scarcely recognizable" in most of our lifetimes.[24]

Already, Hoque points out, freelancers comprise more than one-third of the workforce in the United States, with the trend toward self-employment and entrepreneurship clearly evident in other countries. Uganda, of all places, is a hotbed of economic fluidity, as are Thailand, Brazil, Cameroon, and Vietnam. (Angola, Jamaica, Botswana, Chile, and the Philippines round out the top ten most entrepreneurial countries, according to a survey by UK-based Approved Index.)[25] What is driving this transformation of what constitutes work? Digital technology, of course, as the ways in which we interact with others without regard to time and space continue to be reconceived. For workers, economic fluidity means greater control and autonomy in their lives—an asset cherished by many millennials and post-millennials (or Generation Z).[26] Flexibility is the key reason employers are increasingly attracted to taking on giggers versus full-timers, knowing they can more easily hire and fire as they see fit.

Whether independent contractors, moonlighters, temps, or those working a variety of jobs for a variety of employers, freelancers can fit into the organizational structure of virtually any business, explaining why they have become the poster children for the workforce of the twenty-first century. *Harvard Business Review* labeled this Future Trend "The Rise of the Supertemp" as professionals either downsizing or seeking more independence joined the movement. Fortunately, finding a good match between employer and employee is becoming a lot easier. Students at the Harvard Business School recently developed something called HourlyNerd that hooks up talent with companies, for example, while TaskRabbit is a platform that connects repair people with those needing some kind of home repair or maintenance. ("Help around the home is just a few taps away," goes that company's slogan.)[27]

Considering the trajectory of a world consisting of supertemps leads to nothing short of a revolution in the concept of work. In the next couple of decades, predicts a report issued by the Roosevelt Institute and the Kauffman Foundation, one's career is likely to be made up of a long string of short-term projects rather than doing the same old grind. "By 2040, the job market will consist of part-time assignments, portfolio careers, and entrepreneurialism," according to Slava Solodkiy of medium.com, with a host of implications spinning out of that scenario. The ways in which we prepare for a career will have to be reimagined, for one thing, with the traditional path grounded in formal education no longer necessarily the route to follow. "To be successful," Solidkiy posited, "individuals will have to be more entrepreneurial in thinking and planning their lives, meaning constantly selling themselves, defining one's own work, and educating themselves for future assignments."[28]

Future Trend 17: Fluidity

Decision-Making and Leadership Platform

Implications
Economic fluidity is clearly the model of work in the future.

- It is part of twenty-first-century priorities of resilience and flexibility.

Fluidity is a win-win situation for both employers and employees, at least in theory.

- More planning is required for the model to be successful in the real world.

A global orientation is key for employers and employees alike.

- There are no geographic borders for either talent or gigs.

More professionals will opt out of nine-to-five positions in Corporate America.

- Baby boomers in pursuit of greater freedom and independence will launch "encore" careers.

Values such as stability and predictability will become highly sought after in a fluid economy.

- However flawed, nine-to-five jobs provide a high measure of consistency.

(continued)

Future Trend 17 (*continued*)

Specialization is part and parcel of economic fluidity.

- Generalists are at a competitive disadvantage to those with expertise in any field.

Opportunities
Join the fluid economy.

- Hire freelancers or get hired yourself as an entrepreneur with a portfolio career.

Emphasize control and autonomy when searching for talent.

- Being in charge is the principal asset of working for oneself.

Develop a proprietary gig-based app.

- Use a customized platform to find qualified people in your industry and for your organization.

Train people as supertemps.

- There will be no clear career path as formal education becomes passé or even obsolete.

Borrow the fluidity concept to become a "fluid" organization.

- Seize new opportunities as they arise versus being attached to a particular industry or category.

Adopt alternative, nonlinear forms of organizational structure.

- Hierarchies are less effective in a fluid environment.

Future Trend 18: Disintermediation

The future of business is disintermediated.

—Rachel Croson, Dean, College of Social
Science at Michigan State University

Is there disintermediation in your organization's future? Hopefully not, but it's entirely possible given the ways in which customers are increasingly buying products and services. Disintermediation—the elimination of middlemen as manufacturers or service providers forge a more direct relationship with consumers—is taking the global economic arena by storm as layers and players are removed from what is sometimes called the value chain.[29]

A look at what has taken place in many industries since the late 1990s makes it clear that disintermediation will likely continue to wreak havoc with businesses that are, well, simply minding their own business. Amazon has wiped out thousands of businesses by offering consumers the mother of all one-stop-shops, and the computer biz has gone heavily direct. There are still insurance agents and brokers around, but Geico has made it easy to purchase coverage through its own system. Prepared food is increasingly going direct as marketers such as Hello Fresh and Blue Apron cut out grocery and warehouse stores, with restaurants too beginning to feel the impact of what's now just a blip on the radar. Travel agencies were virtually eliminated once the airlines and other marketers got into the act (corporate clients being the exception), a classic example of how the Internet disrupted consumer behavior at a level equivalent to the invention of electricity more than a century ago.[30]

The key to not being disintermediated, as Paul Morin of the consultancy Company Founder points out, is the degree to which your organization is adding meaningful value to the purchasing process. That's what successful bricks-and-mortar retailers like one's local sporting goods store understand, says Morin, as such businesses "provide a human touch and level of expertise to the transaction that, for now at least, is not easy to replicate online." Prepared food marketers, meanwhile, add value through a compelling brand story, by informing consumers what they should and shouldn't eat in order to stay healthy, and by creating the (correct) impression that there are real people in the company who are passionate about their cause. Being mindful of the market's wants and needs is vital toward differentiating oneself from competitors, he adds, as is providing benefits that consumers truly value.[31]

In her piece for LinkedIn, Rachel Croson lists other examples of why business is speeding toward disintermediation. Uber and AirBNB turned their respective industries on their head by reaching out to consumers directly, and Apple TV is taking the media industry by storm by, in the company's words, "liberating television [by] letting you choose precisely what and when you want to watch." (That company's Apple Pay is similarly messing with the credit card business.) Perhaps the ultimate form of disintermediation is Kickstarter and other crowdfunding sites, where consumers become literally invested in a particular business. Even more interesting is the notion in which an organization itself disintermediates by allowing people to interact with each other rather than follow the traditional (hierarchical) relationship between company and consumer. Finally, microfinance and peer lending groups are challenging banks and venture capitalists in the start-up world, more evidence that disintermediation is gaining traction.[32]

Future Trend 18: Disintermediation

Decision-Making and Leadership Platform

Implications

Industry after industry is becoming disintermediated.

- The middle ground between marketer and consumer is an increasingly dangerous place to be.

Consumers prefer a direct relationship with marketers if they have a choice.

- Fewer layers and players save money and time.

Adding value is essential to the disintermediation equation.

- How does a consumer actually benefit from a direct relationship?

Consumers are well on the way to becoming part of the marketing process.

- Roles are becoming intermingled as barriers between companies and people break down.

Technology, especially mobile, is largely behind disintermediation.

- A direct relationship with marketers is now considered the norm.

More industries, including energy, are heading toward disintermediation.

- Home solar panels, windmills, and even mini-nuclear reactors are becoming more popular.

Opportunities

Disintermediate or be disintermediated.

- Direct relationships between marketers and consumers are coming to your industry soon if they are not already there.

Seek out or invent new ways to forge one-on-one relationships with every customer.

- 1:1 is the ultimate form of marketing.

Strive to add more value to the value chain.

- Examples are good storytelling, information, friendliness, convenience, lower price.

(*continued*)

Future Trend 18 (*continued*)

Turn the tables on the traditional approach to marketing by putting consumers in control.

- Concede power rather than have it taken away from you.

Act as a portal for consumers to interact with each other.

- Serve as the means to establish an authentic brand community.

Invite consumers to own a piece of a business.

- There is no better way than partnerships to establish brand loyalty.

Future Trend 19: E-Commerce

Question of the day: What percentage of total retail sales takes place online? Twenty percent? Thirty percent? Forty percent? Just 8 percent, actually, a figure far below what I had believed based on the hype surrounding e-commerce (and the number of packages arriving at our house courtesy of Amazon Prime). "Not such an eye-popping number," observed letstalkpayments.com upon seeing the latest US Census Bureau data, agreeing that general perceptions regarding online retail significantly exceeded reality.[33] One might think that most bricks-and-mortar stores had gone the way of Virgin Megastores and Blockbuster or would very soon, and that anyone thinking of opening a traditional retail business was loony.

Despite the high probability that selling and buying something in the real world will always be possible, the fact is that e-commerce is gradually growing and will, I believe, become the dominant form of retail. E-commerce is, after all, grounded in the same kind of thinking that is driving other economic Future Trends, such as personalization, microbranding, disintermediation, and the rise of electronic money. Going back a decade from 2016, e-commerce business tripled to reach $100 billion a year, hardly chump change regardless of its relatively low percentage of total retail sales.[34] As significant, e-commerce is not just increasing but mutating, with mobile catching up fast to non-mobile online transactions. Having grown up with mobile devices as baby boomers did with television and the Greatest Generation did with radio, post-millennials will look first to their smartphones, tablets, and whatever gizmo comes next for everything, including shopping. E-commerce is destined to greatly accelerate as connectivity becomes less expensive and more people own smartphones.

E-commerce is currently growing at about 10 percent annually (about three times higher than total retail), but bigger things are literally in store as new products and services are introduced into the mix. Amazon is rapidly becoming the Sears, Roebuck of the twenty-first century, with drone delivery and a "try-on service" just a couple of ways it is pushing into new businesses. "E-commerce will truly become the future of retail, as nearly all of the growth in the retail sector now takes place in the digital space," predicts BI Intelligence.[35]

It's also easy to be bullish on e-commerce as more marketers establish digs online and build what Jason Trout of ShoppinPal and others call omnichannel experiences. Retailers' apps, such as that of Crate & Barrel, can cross over various mobile devices and browsers, making shopping more convenient. Providing a "seamless customer experience" is the goal, whereby consumers can shift their shopping from online to in-store and vice versa. iPad-equipped store associates, like those the UK fashion retailer Oasis carry, is another way the real and virtual worlds are being fused to give shoppers what they want and avoid lines at checkout. Starbucks has made getting caffeinated a simpler proposition through its various channels, and cosmetics retailer Sephora has a devoted following due to its technology-enabled "My Beauty Bag" program. Finally, Chipotle is blazing the seamless, multichannel trail to get customers' favorite burrito into their hands pronto, another example of the wave of the future.[36] "Businesses are not just focusing on a digital store selling some nice-enough items, but instead they're trying to create new markets, plug the unexplored terrains, create a shopping experience that consumers can enjoy as they browse, provide round-the-clock services, and meet the overall customer service expectations at all times," noted Saad Khan, founder and CEO of the shopping platform Whoopey.com, capturing the essence of this Future Trend.[37]

Future Trend 19: E-Commerce

Decision-Making and Leadership Platform

Implications

E-Commerce is currently a relatively small piece of the total retail pie.

- Online business is still in the relatively early stage of development.

Traditional retail will not be replaced by e-tail.

- Leading marketers are proving that the two are not only not mutually exclusive but synergistic.

(continued)

Future Trend 19 (*continued*)

The only significant growth in retail is coming from e-commerce.

- E-tailers are stealing existing shoppers and attracting new ones through innovative technologies.

Generational dynamics are playing a major role in the growth of e-commerce.

- Many more e-shoppers will emerge as the older population ages out.

Seamless omnichannel experiences are pointing to the future of e-commerce.

- The goal is to allow consumers to shop anywhere, anytime, with any device.

The day is coming in which we will not differentiate between online and real worlds.

- Physical and virtual realities will be blended and meshed together into everyday life.

Opportunities
Open up your e-store.

- Make it a complement to your traditional business located in the material world.

Capitalize on emerging technologies in building or expanding an e-commerce platform.

- Build in alternative ordering, payment, and delivery systems.

Think first of potential consumer benefits when designing an e-commerce model.

- What are the ways in which a shopper can save time and/or money?

Aim for the shopping experience to be an integral part of a product's or service's reason for being.

- Again, the journey is becoming seen as more important than the destination.

(*continued*)

Future Trend 19 (*continued*)

Focus on differentiation within the purchasing process itself.

- The new kind of shopping environment mandates meaningful points of distinction at all levels.

Exploit technologies in order to offer consumers greater customization and personalization.

- Use the predictive power of data to predetermine preferences.

Future Trend 20: Analogism

For every trend there is a backlash or countertrend, they say, a sentiment with which I agree heartily. Trends tend to bounce off each other in a reactionary manner, with no better example than the love-hate relationship between digital and analog. The further we go down the technological rabbit hole, one could say, the deeper we crave genuine, authentic, and sensory experiences found only in the real world. Information in bits and bytes is all well and good, but there is no substitute for that which is palpable, visceral, and corporal (i.e., of the body). Humans are craving analog or physical experiences of all kinds, a direct response to ever-increasing technology in our lives. Analogism—the backlash against the encroachment of digital universes manifested as a longing for humanistic experiences—will flourish in the years ahead, making life a kind of schizophrenic existence located somewhere between virtuality and reality.

Already we can see the emergence of analogism as a reaction to (or perhaps resistance against) our seemingly endless screen watching. Millennials, of all people, appear to be driving this Future Trend, with some primitive urge to be immersed in alternative sensory environments possibly operating in their iBrains. Making one's computer keyboard sound like an old typewriter has become a thing with some younger people (who have never actually typed on an Underwood or Remington, it need be said), for example, and the classic Bell telephone ring is a popular choice on an iPhone's sound setting.[38] Some consider the phenomenon to be just about retro or nostalgia, but I look at it as much more than a yearning for the past. Analogism works at a primal level, I believe, appealing to something that is cognitively hardwired and DNA-encoded.

You name it—LPs and turntables, film photography (including Polaroid cameras), and, believe it or not, books made out of actual paper—are part of the analog wave that continues to gain size and power as it rolls along.

"Analog has never been so popular," notes dw.com, citing Amazon's plans to open a physical bookstore in Manhattan (and acquisition of Whole Foods) as evidence that the digital world is not enough. Nokia has rereleased its iconic 3310 phone, which originally debuted in 2000, illustrating the speed in which the new becomes the old within the universe of technology. While our chip-laden devices no doubt allow us to do things previous generations could not even imagine, something is clearly missing from them, this accounting for the popularity of analog. Digital is basically unisensory while analog is multisensory, with touch and even smell often part of the latter's appeal. Holding and playing a vinyl record is a much different, more emotional experience from clicking on a downloaded music file, this tactility at the root of it all. Next time at your local café, notice how many twentysomethings are writing in their journals in, yes, longhand, an art form that very well may not be taught in school for much longer.[39] Calligraphy and music made on acoustic instruments are also making comebacks, making one wonder if more artistic forms from medieval times are heading our way soon.[40]

No one understands this Future Trend better than David Sax, author of *The Revenge of Analog: Real Things and Why They Matter.* "A funny thing happened on the way to the digital utopia," he writes in the book, declaring that "we've begun to fall back in love with the very analog goods and ideas the tech gurus insisted that we no longer needed."[41] Indeed, while the cloud is a magical thing, people need to have their feet on the ground, ensuring there will be a bright and shiny future for all things real.

Future Trend 20: Analogism

Decision-Making and Leadership Platform

Implications
Analogism is a direct reply to encroaching technology.

- Smart devices are not satisfying our need for physical, sensory, and emotional experiences.

The constant parade of the "next new thing" is literally desensitizing us.

- Thousands of years of immersion in an analog world is catching up with us in our digital age.

There is a symbiotic relationship between analog and digital.

- The relationship is an interdependent, mutually beneficial connection that is fueling each other.

(*continued*)

Future Trend 20 (*continued*)

Marketers are smartly focusing on millennials with analog products.

- Digital natives are ironically most attracted to non-digital things and experiences.

Digital marketers are paradoxically most attuned to the analog opportunity.

- Techies are most aware of the holes in technology.

Hipness and kitsch are part of the appeal of analogism.

- Old is always cooler than new as the new becomes old instantly.

Opportunities

Mine the rich territory that is analogism.

- Satisfy consumers' urge for what is perceived as real, genuine, and authentic.

Approach analogism as a means to stand out from the ceaseless march of technology.

- An example is Seth Godin's "purple cow" in a field of monochrome Holsteins.

Reintroduce iconic products and services from the past.

- Include things from a generation or two ago that left a cultural imprint.

Offer consumers sensory experiences unavailable in contemporary technology.

- Sights, sounds, smells, tastes, and feels are steeped in memory.

Blend advanced technologies with retro to create interesting, unique combinations of new and old.

- Use digital interpretations of analog artifacts.

Target millennials and post-millennials with analog efforts.

- Those generations perceive anything from the pre-digital age as foreign, alien, and somehow cool.

CHAPTER THREE

~

Political Trends

A half-century after Coca-Cola's iconic commercial envisioning the world being taught to sing in perfect harmony, the global geopolitical landscape remains a cacophonous affair. The worse news is that things do not appear to be getting better, making any realistic vision of the future a rather gloomy one. While there are some positive signs—the breakdown of monolithic authoritarian institutions, the ascendant power of a more informed, connected citizenship, and a growing movement dedicated to preserving the planet and its inhabitants, to name a few—it's clear that the third rock from the sun is becoming an increasingly scarier place to call home. Rather than becoming more flat, as Thomas Friedman suggested in his influential book of 2005, globalization appears to be making our world more uneven and dangerous. Earth may indeed be getting smaller as technology brings us closer together but, rather than ushering in a new age of peace through empathy or commonality, its metaphoric shrinking is creating more chaos and volatility.

The ten Future Trends in this chapter reflect the rockier geopolitical terrain that lies before us. The trends of instability and populism are understandably making us feel that we are standing on shaky ground, while the trends of discontinuities, rogueism, and disintegration are contributing to a budding anti-politics movement. Over the next couple of decades, politics is destined to become more complex and unpredictable, I argue, a function of more competitors vying for recognition and power. The post–Cold War political universe has devolved into a Babel-like struggle for attention, leaving many of us dazed and confused or, in different cinematic terms, with a growing sense of cultural vertigo. While a greater number of people have the opportunity to make their voices heard—a good thing in theory—the election of an outsider is hardly a guarantee for good political leadership, something already being seen in various countries.

Happily, however, the party-based system that has ruled for centuries in many nations' politics is likely to continue to be tossed into the dustbin of history. Smaller groups are banding together to form new political alliances and coalitions, a positive development in that they more effectively address citizens' concerns rather than attempt to represent an all-encompassing ideology (e.g., liberal or conservative). Here in the United States, the nearly constant challenge for both the Democrats and the Republicans to reinvent themselves due to a loss of identity reflects the reality that such macro-parties no longer reflect the way voters approach politics. Information technology is serving as a great equalizer, with only a laptop and an Internet connection all one really needs to start a political movement. As in all other arenas of life, the top-down is being overthrown by the bottom-up, a topsy-turvying that will serve as a primary theme in our world of tomorrow.

The meaning of all this is clear for organizations of all stripes: business is no longer really a separate entity from politics, with the two pursuits sharing an increasingly symbiotic relationship. (One might even propose a linguistic merger of the pair such as "poli-business.") In the future, businesspeople will require greater fluency in the world of politics, and politicians will need to be more conversant in the language of business. The even greater challenge for managers is how to anticipate future events in an environment in which the only constant is change. If there is one thing to be learned from a long view of history, it is the continually escalating pace of society and the exponential acceleration of change, something that will no doubt hold true for the remainder of the twenty-first century. Thought leadership is more and more reliant on having a clear and compelling vision of the future, a fitting way to begin this chapter.

Future Trend 21: Instability

The world has been politically instable since the days of cave dwellers, of course, but the presence of billions of people on the planet and the development of weapons far more powerful than clubs is making tensions in our cave run a lot higher. "State fragility and ideological conflicts all threaten to increase instability in the coming decades," foresees the Futures Centre, thinking that this geopolitical wobbliness "will have important implications for global trade, migration, governance and even population growth, as well as human well-being."[1] Terrorism—including that increasingly taking place online—is just one contributing factor to the feeling that the world could go kablooey at any moment, and that there does not seem to be any good solution to the problem compounds a general sense of helplessness or lack of control.

The perception that geopolitics are getting ever shakier is borne out by hard numbers. Between 2008 and 2015, the average Global Peace Index (GPI) country score fell 2.4 percent, the Institute of Economics and Peace (IEP) reported in 2015, data indicating that the world has indeed become a more perilous place. (The mere fact there is a "peace index" can be taken as a disturbing sign of the times; it serves as a reminder that some degree of international conflict is essentially inevitable.) Even worse news is that there is a correlation between economics and geopolitical instability; since 2008, the total economic effect of some form of violence on the global economy has increased by 15 percent, according to the IEP, an impact that translates to more than 13 percent of the world's gross domestic product in 2014 dollars.[2]

Geopolitical instability can take many forms, adding to the sensation that one is standing on shakier and shakier ground. Spats between nations, a constant flow of refugees fleeing intolerable conditions, and turbulent financial markets are commonplace, and there is a greater reluctance for the United States to play global cop or get involved in sticky situations abroad as it used to.[3] Everyone was on pins and needles during the postwar era, but the Cold War between the two superpowers was a much simpler model of international conflict than the one we have today. Every day another splinter group hostile to the West seems to emerge, each one's version of radical politics hard for people of democratic nations to understand, much less combat. As well, regimes are continually changing, making it difficult to even remember which countries are on our side and which are not. It's thus not surprising that most leading futurists believe that geopolitical instability will intensify over the next two decades, as there is little evidence to suggest otherwise.

To their credit, more businesspeople are recognizing that geopolitical instability is something they must increasingly take into account. "Executives are likelier than ever to believe that geopolitical and domestic political instability will affect global business and their own companies in coming years," a recent McKinsey Global Survey on globalization reported, with twice the number of respondents saying it was a "very important" trend versus just a couple of years ago. McKinsey calls the trend "geostrategic risks," something that executives sensibly believe will likely negatively impact their organizations. Very few respondents to the survey said they were doing anything about these risks, however, feeling perhaps that such machinations were simply beyond their control.[4] Given that, how can businesspeople best manage the trend, one should ask, and even possibly use it to their advantage?

Future Trend 21: Instability

Decision-Making and Leadership Platform

Implications
Many of us are experiencing a growing sense of cultural vertigo as the geopolitical climate becomes wobblier.

- There is less clarity between the good and bad guys and even what constitutes goodness and badness.

There is an inescapable feeling that it's an increasingly dangerous world.

- Greater risks appear to be out there from both known and unknown enemies.

The flux in global politics is trickling down to the local level.

- There is nowhere to hide in a smaller, more connected world.

A craving for a sense of constancy and permanence is common.

- It reflects the basic human need to feel safe and secure.

The transience of political structures will encourage people to look elsewhere for guidance.

- A broader distribution of power will allow non-political organizations to demonstrate leadership qualities.

Products and services offering a sense of solidity are likely to be welcomed in the future.

- Stable brands may serve as surrogates for unstable nations and states.

Opportunities
Claim industry territory as a known entity in an increasingly complex and uncertain world.

- Convey ideas of assurance and certainty.

Offer consumers ballast in the stormy political seas.

- Prioritize values of trust, reliability, and dependability in brand messaging and deliverables.

(continued)

Future Trend 21 (*continued*)

Avoid overtly political stances in marketing efforts.

- Any form of partisanship will be a limiting factor.

Adopt truthfulness and honesty as your corporate mantra.

- Embrace such traits that transcend here-today, gone-tomorrow political bodies.

Emphasize experience and history in corporate communications.

- Tell true stories that demonstrate diligence and perseverance.

Position your brands as partners in it for the long run.

- Form committed relationships that consumers can rely on in good and bad times.

Future Trend 22: Populism

Can you say "Trump" or "Brexit"? The last presidential election and the UK's exit from the EU were each much about citizens' loss of faith and trust in their respective governments, a movement that is global in scope and indicative of where politics is headed in the future. The passion surrounding presidential candidate Bernie Sanders was also rooted in populist sentiment, and ParlGov data has tracked a recent surge in voting for populist candidates in dozens of other countries.[5] Populism—appealing to or support for the concerns of ordinary people—is about the rejection of officially recognized government bodies and the nomination of outside-the-system individuals and groups to leadership positions. Populism is part of the larger shift away from macro-institutional concentrations of power as people seek out ways to gain more control in their personal lives. A guerilla model of politics is on the cusp of usurping the traditional structure grounded in bureaucracy and elitism, with outliers better positioned than professionals to get elected and stay in office.

Although pundits disagree about whether populism is a good or bad thing (most seem to believe it is a dangerous trend that carries significant risks because of its leanings toward xenophobia—something borne out by history), there is a consensus that there is something about it that resonates on a deep, emotional level among a large and growing segment of people all over the world. "Characterized by a suspicion and hostility toward elites, mainstream politics, and established institutions," reads the 2017 National Intelligence Council's Global Trends Report, populism "reflects rejection of the economic effects of globalization and frustration with the responses of political and economic elites to the public's concerns."[6] Perhaps the most potent aspect of populism is its bipartisanship (i.e., that it can be equally appealing to both the right and left wing). The notion of a de-politicized form of politics is indeed a powerful one.

What is driving populism, and why is it going to intensify in the years ahead? One word: change. Populism "can best be explained as a cultural backlash in Western societies against long-term, ongoing social change," posited Pippa Norris of Harvard University in a 2016 article in the *Washington Post*, with those resistant to rising gender and sexual fluidity, diversity, and secularism making their voices heard.[7] But if there is only one constant in life, it is change, meaning that populism is likely to escalate as traditionalists push back against the continual blurring of gender, ethnic, racial, and religious lines. Technological advances too promise to fuel populism as machines replace more workers. Unemployment triggered by the digital divide is ideal fodder for disgruntled citizens to blame those in power for the problem, and to look to charismatic figures claiming to know how to fix it. Almost half of the jobs in the United States alone are at risk of being automated, according to a 2013 Oxford University study, with robots, artificial intelligence, and drones likely to put many out of work.[8]

Given the tremendous amount of change that will take place over the next two or three decades, businesspeople should be prepared for a world in which populist thought and action is a fact of life. Populism is likely to spill over from politics to other arenas of everyday life including the marketplace, making one wonder whether and how it can be leveraged. As populism expands, large, powerful companies may be at risk of being perceived as not in synch with the interests of ordinary folks, a proposition that demands new and different kinds of thinking.

Future Trend 22: Populism

Decision-Making and Leadership Platform

Implications

There is a good chance that the concept of populism will spread well beyond politics.

- "Officialdom" will be perceived by many as more of a liability than an asset.

Corporations and larger brands are an undeniable part of the global economic system.

- Potential risks exist in being viewed by populists as established, elitist institutions.

People and organizations deemed to be "outside the system" will wield considerable power on that basis alone.

- "Everyman-ness" of populism will be an increasingly valuable asset.

Populism is potentially a global business strategy given its ubiquity.

- Support for the concerns of ordinary people is functioning like an ideological Esperanto.

Siding with "ordinary" people or the "common man" is a time-tested political technique.

- Populism serves as a rare opportunity to reach a mass audience in business as well.

Populism is a careful line to walk because of xenophobia and intolerance embedded in some of its versions.

- History shows how populism can fall well short of being of and for the people.

Opportunities

Tap into the passion driving populism.

- The perception of being an underdog is a compelling proposition.

(*continued*)

Future Trend 22 (*continued*)

Position relevant brands as populist to appeal to consumers' desire to align themselves with outside-the-system interests.

- Present products and services as for the people, by the people.

Emphasize traditional values in those brands with a proud past.

- Tell consumers that "some things never change and that's a good thing."

Trade on populist sentiment in communications for outlier brands.

- Adopt antiestablishment values in the philosophy and messaging of renegade products and services.

Use guerilla marketing tactics to reinforce a non-elitist image.

- Prioritize flexibility, resourcefulness, and the element of surprise over artillery power.

Tread carefully with any and all populist campaigns.

- Employ the concept while avoiding real politics and actual politicians.

Future Trend 23: Coalitions

As global geopolitics crumbles into a million little pieces, a new model of relationships between people is emerging. Coalitions—partnerships and alliances grounded in shared ideologies that cross social, economic, and geographic boundaries—are busting out all over as politics as we knew it becomes history. Coalitions are the natural result of a greater fluidity of ideas due to the march of technology and the erosion of borders. As communities of interest, coalitions are destined to flourish in the future as the law of particle physics applies. Large objects moving at high speed tend to break up, that law states, a scientific metaphor for what is beginning to take place all around the world. Chinua Achebe, the African novelist, said it best (borrowing a line from a Yeats poem): things fall apart and, over time, the center cannot hold, a nice way to describe world events in the twenty-first century.

Recent political goings-on may suggest that liberals and conservatives are heading in opposite directions, but experts recognize that the long-term trend is coalitions, sometimes between seemingly strange bedfellows. What wonks call "transpartisanship" is likely to trump, so to speak, a polarized political climate, with common ground being found across party lines on issues like criminal justice, climate change, and access to health care. Even in the United States, a country that pundits consider historically politically divided, is home to this new kind of coalition building. "Devising work-arounds to move new policies, defend existing ones, or simply re-open lines of communication are happening," the political reform organization New America asserts, thinking "this is the future of American policymaking."[9]

Coalitions represent a key Future Trend not just in the United States but globally. The Policy Network, an international think tank and political network, goes so far as to call coalitions "the party of the future," and believes they symbolize a new form of politics. The erosion of class consciousness and decline of trade unions are just a couple of factors to spark the rise of coalitions, with mainstream political parties in many nations increasingly seen by voters as clunky relics of the past.[10] Most interesting, even though proposed policy change is often part of the agenda, coalitions are not really about politics. Rather, coalitions are about ideas, something that pays no heed to social, economic, and geographic barriers. The old guard will resist any and all challenges to its system, of course, as major power is at stake, but a freer exchange and sharing of ideas is the wave of the future, regardless of how much money citizens have or where they live.

For businesspeople, the rise of coalitions presents important potential consequences. In a larger sense, the gradual breakdown of the simplistic left/right model of politics suggests that the ways in which consumers have been sorted into buckets based on their supposed values are less and less reliable. Political affiliation has served as a primary means of categorizing consumers, but it now represents an outdated approach to parsing what makes people tick. Traditional market segmentation techniques no longer apply, in other words, meaning that managers must look to different ways to view and find consumers and customers. Increasingly, the communities to which one belongs define one's identity and point to what kind of products and services one is likely to be interested in. How should marketers think about coalitions, and how can they tap into their power as they become recognized as a central guiding force in people's lives?

Future Trend 23: Coalitions

Decision-Making and Leadership Platform

Implications

The acceleration of everyday life is helping to trigger the breakup of large political institutions.

- The center of anything of considerable mass cannot hold at high speed.

Coalitions will become increasingly significant and influential in the future.

- Partnerships and alliances grounded in shared ideas are ascending in power.

Universal issues will serve as the primary currency of coalitions.

- They are passion points that potentially affect all citizens of the globe.

Demographics is no longer a particularly good way of categorizing people.

- Common interests > age, race, ethnicity, etc.

It is imperative for all marketers to view consumers from a global perspective.

- Coalitions will cross geographic borders with reckless abandon.

Economic measures such as income or net worth are increasingly less relevant for many product categories.

- Beliefs transcend money for basic commodities.

Opportunities

Look to powerful coalitions versus political parties to read the global cultural climate.

- Group sentiment is a more precise indicator of consumers' attitudes at any given time.

Treat coalitions as a legitimate target audience with whom to connect.

- Create custom messaging tailored to members' respective shared interests.

(continued)

Future Trend 23 (*continued*)

Forge coalitions as a kind of brand community.

- Package content that members will find interesting and informative.

View consumers through the lens of "transpartisanship."

- Promote brand values that virtually everybody can relate to and rally around.

Be a champion of open lines of communications.

- Transparency is the modus operandi of coalitions.

Support causes that are universal in scope.

- Use social responsibility to identify a large group of consumers who are passionate about a particular issue.

Future Trend 24: Discontinuities

Peter Drucker said it a little less than a half-century ago. We're living in "the age of discontinuity," the business guru argued in a book of that name, seeing social change as the defining element of our times. "The closing decades of the twentieth century have been characterized as a period of disruption and discontinuity in which the structure and meaning of economy, polity, and society have been radically altered," the description of the book first published in 1969 read, citing a leap of new technologies, transformation to a global economy, rise of pluralistic institutions, and greater dependency on knowledge as the key shapers of this new age.[11] Over the past fifty years, discontinuity—sudden breaks in governing bodies resulting in new and different kinds of cultural configurations—has only intensified as a political, economic, and social force, and is almost certain to continue to escalate over the next few decades.

One person picking up where Drucker left off is W. P. S. Sidhu of the Brookings Institution India Center. Sidhu sees increasing overall wealth, an aging population, climate change, spread of the online universe, artificial intelligence, automation, and a more complex geopolitical landscape as the major drivers of twenty-first-century discontinuities. For Sidhu and others, a "more disorderly world" appears to be inevitable as disruption in various forms becomes business as usual. The possibility of "black swan" events—

worst-case scenarios often with apocalyptic consequences such as nuclear war—are especially disturbing, but reflect the range of disturbances that are likely in our collective future. International organizations such as the United Nations will have less influence in the future age of discontinuities, with the private sector and local governments to hold more sway.[12]

All one needs to do to get a good sense of the potential discontinuities looming in front of us is to read the very first page of the World Economic Forum's *Global Risks Report 2017* (twelfth edition). That page consists of a Risks-Trends Interconnections Map that charts out in (scary) detail five different kinds of risks—Economic, Geopolitical, Societal, Technological, and Environmental. A host of global bummers—rising urbanization, extreme weather events, state collapse, large-scale involuntary migration, cyber-attacks, fiscal crises, shifting power, and more—are possible, the map shows, with one big one—profound social instability—lurking smack-dab in the middle like a spider in its web. Risks are rated on measures of both likelihood and impact, with extreme weather events coming in first on the former list and weapons of mass destruction ranking number one on the latter. The global community is facing "the threat of a less cooperative, more inward-looking world," wrote Klaus Schwab, the founder and executive chair of the World Economic Forum, in his preface to the report, thinking that we are at a "pivotal moment" in history.[13]

How should businesspeople react to such disconcerting forecasts, and what steps should they take in the case that such discontinuities unfold? Clearly, sticking one's head in the sand is a bad idea given the possible impact of many potential events, meaning outlining action steps to take in long-range planning is a wise move indeed. More broadly, it makes sense to simply assume that we will be living in an age heavily defined by discontinuity in the future, and that the kind of social change that Drucker wrote about in 1969 will be on steroids over the next few decades. Those organizations best equipped to adapt to sudden change are most likely to thrive, we can safely assume, suggesting that resiliency and flexibility will be key attributes to possess in the years ahead.

Future Trend 24: Discontinuities

Decision-Making and Leadership Platform

Implications

Sharp twists and turns are the new world order.

- Life will be a wild roller coaster ride for the foreseeable future.

Instability (Future Trend 21) is the root cause of discontinuities.

- Geopolitical turmoil is directly correlated with unpredictability.

Technology, globalism, pluralism, and knowledge are driving change.

- These are the same factors as in 1969 but in a much different geo-political context.

Experts agree that a large number and wide range of discontinuities are possible.

- Disruptions are the natural result of a more disorderly world.

Corporations will wield more power than multilateral institutions in averting and managing discontinuities.

- The private sector is gaining in strength as the public sector weakens.

Agility—the ability to bend without breaking and/or to adapt to new situations—will be a greater determinant of success.

- It is incumbent upon businesses to become more elastic and pliable.

Opportunities

Build mechanisms of adaptability into your organizational system and corporate culture.

- Create a strategic apparatus to quickly change course as discontinuities pop up.

Make scenario planning a staple of your annual planning process.

- Outline actions to take should "what if" situations develop.

(continued)

Future Trend 24 (*continued*)

Expect "a more connected, heterogeneous world in which information is power."

- Explore how potential disruptions can interfere with this paradigm.

Seek out partnerships that can help lessen the negative impact of discontinuities.

- Local governments, utilities, and media will be especially useful.

Pursue continuity but expect discontinuity.

- Hoping for the best but preparing for the worst is a reasonable philosophy to put into practice.

Consider brand strategies based in the concept of discontinuity.

- Disruptiveness has proven to be an effective marketing technique.

Future Trend 25: Rogueism

Twenty years in the future, America perches on the edge of collapse, devastated by drought and dwindling resources. California, now a totalitarian surveillance state controlling the lion's share of the nation's economy, is on the brink of secession.[14]

So goes the teaser for *Rogue State*, one installment of Steven Konkoly's popular "Fractured State" series of books categorized as "speculative post-apocalyptic thrillers." As we all know, however, truth is stranger than fiction, making the real future an even scarier proposition should some of today's more troubling trends continue along their current trajectory. Actual rogue states are popping up with increasing frequency around the world or at least appear to be, creating the inescapable feeling that the emerging geopolitical climate is indeed a precarious one.

The term "rogue states" (nations that play by their own rules, essentially) became popular in the 1980s to describe those countries that did not fall neatly into the bipolar, superpower-based model of the Cold War. "The term 'rogue states' entered the U.S. foreign policy lexicon after the Cold War to designate regimes that employed terrorism as an instrument of state policy and attempted to acquire weapons of mass destruction in pursuit of policy goals," explains the Wilson Center, the core group at that time being Iraq, Libya, Iran, and North Korea.[15] After the fall of the Soviet Union in 1991, the phrase began to refer to states that were determined to disrupt the existing world order (although Bill Clinton preferred the term "outlaw nation").

Today, rogue states are playing an even more important role on the global stage, a trend that will likely accelerate as large governing bodies continue to break down. In the future, however, what we can call "rogueism" is destined to go far beyond politics, I believe, by evolving into a philosophy or, more simply, a way of seeing the world or approaching life. Rogueism has been heavily imprinted with evilness, of course, a function of dictatorships run by apparently crazy despots who just want to mess with the bigger powers as a means of exerting their own influence. But "going rogue," as that phrase goes, isn't necessarily a bad thing, and it is this idea that I think will spread like wildfire over the next couple of decades. Rogueism—exhibiting maverick-like behavior or bucking the status quo—is actually turning out to be a good thing, with displays of independence or going "off-script" taken as signs that one thinks and acts for oneself rather than behaving like a sheep or lemming.

Businesspeople can learn a lot from the notion of going rogue (which, long before Sarah Palin used it as the title of her 2009 memoir, was meant to describe elephants that went wild and became violent). For managers of all kinds of organizations, rogueism implies that one's company will not follow the rules of a particular industry or product category and, if the situation calls for it, will mess with the big guys to carve out a niche in an increasingly competitive and global marketplace. When you think about it, disrupting the existing world order is precisely what many brands are or should be about, with almost all companies to benefit from having at least a little outlaw in them. As in politics, playing it safe by staking out a centrist position in the business world is likely a losing strategy; it is the outliers and risk-takers who are winning the day through innovative ideas and bold actions.

Future Trend 25: Rogueism

Decision-Making and Leadership Platform

Implications
Rogueism will lose many of its evil connotations in the future.

- A new and improved version grounded in nonconformity will emerge.

Populist political movements are a kinder, gentler form of rogueism.

- People everywhere are seemingly tired of the same old, same old.

(continued)

Future Trend 25 (*continued*)

Rogueness is a universal concept that translates across time and space.

- Resistance to the status quo can be found in all societies.

Playing by one's own rules is actually a very American idea.

- Rogueism reflects our cherished, revolutionary values of independence, freedom, and liberty.

More individuals and organizations will embrace elements of rogueness.

- Unorthodox behavior usually offers some kind of competitive advantage.

Rogueism is a key ingredient in the business strategy of "disruption."

- Chaos is a proven way to get people's attention.

Opportunities

Go rogue by stirring up some chaos in your industry or product category.

- Play by an alternative set of rules to capture consumers' attention.

Position or reposition appropriate brands as outlaws.

- Appeal to consumers' bad boy or bad girl fantasies.

Throw some unpredictability and volatility into your business plans and corporate culture.

- Zag when your competitors zig.

Mess with the big guys as a means of exerting your influence.

- Distract 'em if you can't beat 'em.

Look for opportunities to disrupt normalcy and regularity.

- Break existing patterns and deviate from expectations.

Stake out your territory in the margins or fringes of the marketplace.

- Avoid mainstream, middle-of-the-road thinking and action whenever and wherever possible.

Future Trend 26: E-government

Which country's government is currently the most technologically advanced? The United States? Japan? China? Chances are you didn't say Estonia, the country in the Baltic region of northern Europe that used to be part of the Soviet Union. Although it has about the population of Maine, Estonia is a trailblazer in e-government (i.e., the "use of information technology to support government operations, engage citizens, and provide government services," as the University at Albany Center for Technology in Government [UACTG] defines the term).[16] Estonians are able to vote online and receive their refunds just a couple of days after filing their taxes, just a few things many Americans could only wish for. Estonia's government is so wired that some experts refer to the country as a start-up, quite an amazing thing given the seemingly antediluvian workings of your typical public institution.[17]

Estonia represents the future of government, which is becoming increasingly digitized in virtually all countries around the world. E-government includes four basic areas, according to the UACTG: e-services ("the electronic delivery of government information, programs, and services"); e-democracy ("the use of electronic communications to increase citizen participation in the public decision-making process"); e-commerce ("the electronic exchange of money for goods and services"); and e-management ("the use of information technology to improve the management of government"). While Estonia is far ahead of the curve, some other countries, states, and cities (including New York City, with its NYC.GOV) are embracing the e-government concept with mostly positive results.[18]

It may be taking longer than in other arenas, but politics is also gradually transforming into an online model that points to how government will be run in the future. E-politics (or electronic politics) is another part of the Internetization of government, a trend that continues to pick up speed as more people gain access to digital technologies. Some experts are hailing E-politics as a "great equalizer" that will eventually shift government from a "top-down" institution to a "bottom-up" one by giving, as the 1960s anthem went, "power to the people." E-politics is also seen as being much more "open source" than the traditional version, with transparency and collaboration at the heart of this new model.[19] All elements of the political process appear to be heading online, with social media platforms to obviously play a central role in how people get elected and what they do once they are in office.

According to Hana Francisco and Carly Olson, e-politics began in 2004 when Democratic presidential candidate Howard Dean hosted a blog in which he communicated directly with those following his campaign. Social media played a key part of Barack Obama's 2008 campaign for president, and in 2012 he announced his candidacy for reelection via an e-mail to supporters. Facebook and Twitter were essential elements of that campaign, tools that both Hillary Clinton and Donald Trump used extensively in their own respective runs for the presidency in 2016.[20] President Trump and his staff are avid Tweeters, of course, taking e-politics to an entirely new level. Trump breaks a cardinal rule of social media by not interacting with his followers, but it can't be denied that he's taking e-politics in a new and interesting direction. E-politics and e-government are clearly the future of the public sector, and something from which the private sector can and should learn.

Future Trend 26: E-government

Decision-Making and Leadership Platform

Implications

E-governments are coming, whether we like it or not.

- Get ready for digital national identities, Orwellian forms of centralization, and even global citizenship.

There are clear positives associated with e-government and e-politics.

- The usual conveniences and efficiencies of online technology will be realized.

There are also clear negatives associated with e-government and e-politics.

- The usual privacy issues and dehumanization of online technology should be expected.

Government and politics will be increasingly interwoven with social media.

- The public sector is morphing into a kind of social network.

The best potential benefit of e-government: more direct communication between elected officials and individual citizens.

- This model is closer to the democratic principle of "We the people."

The traditional markers of government will gradually disappear.

- Buildings, such as state capitols, will become more symbolic than operative.

(continued)

Future Trend 26 (*continued*)

Opportunities
"E" your company and brands.

- Seize the advantages of an online model.

Accentuate the positives of digitalization.

- Examples are speed, consumer engagement and empowerment, relationship-building and collaborations.

Eliminate the negatives of digitalization.

- Ensure that there is no "ghost in the machine" (i.e., the dehumanization that is common to technology).

Approach "e-ness" as a tool of democracy.

- Use technology as a great equalizer versus divider.

View your organization as a start-up.

- Build your entire business around the concept of an entrepreneurial venture committed to fast growth and innovation.

Embrace the idea of "open source" in your marketing efforts.

- Invite consumers to help map your brands' respective journeys.

Future Trend 27: Grassroots

"The future of politics is grassroots," wrote Joshua Habursky and Mike Fulton in the *Washington Post* in 2017, a logical conclusion after witnessing citizens' direct involvement in recent elections.[21] Grassroots—the participation of people in an organization or movement, usually at a local or basic level—was traditionally considered a nice complement to a political campaign, adding a populist dimension to the process. But now the cart is leading the horse, one may say, as millions of voters lead demonstrations, attend town hall meetings, and give time and money to candidates and causes in whom they believe. Politics has become more about citizens' passions than the individual running for office, a fortuitous turning of the tables that, at least in theory, gives more power to the people.

Although grassroots is a relatively new political trend, history is definitely on its side. Grassroots activism is at the very heart of the Founding Fathers' radical concept of "We the people," suggesting that it is a revolutionary development almost two and a half centuries in the making. Best of all, grassroots thinking and doing are not just consistent with our democratic ideals but appear to actually shape the political process, media coverage, and public sentiment, making it a powerful, multipartisan force that potentially represents a new model of citizenship. "Americans of all demographics are more poised now than ever to take action and to get involved at all levels of government," Habursky and Fulton continued, seeing the next stage as being the formation of "meaningful outlets to exert this collective influence and creative strategies to maximize their effectiveness."[22]

It is hardly coincidental, of course, that grassroots politics has come into its own in the age of social media. A couple of centuries ago, grassroots politics consisted largely of a concerned citizen making a speech on a tree stump in a park or public square. Oration was the favored method of communication, an ardent but not very efficient means of persuasion. With Facebook and other social networks, the politically inclined can now share their thoughts with thousands, perhaps millions of people around the world in real time, a hugely powerful way to potentially shape public opinion. Indeed, the Pew Research Center found that 20 percent of users of social media altered their opinion on a particular issue based on information read online, and that 17 percent of users changed their position regarding a specific candidate running for office.[23] The reach of social media has made "Think Global, Act Local" much more than a groovy expression, turning grassroots advocacy from a bunch of people holding up signs into a worldwide movement dedicated to the interests of the people at large.

What does the flourishing of grassroots politics suggest on a more macro level, and what does it mean for businesspeople? Grassroots is not just a political philosophy or tactic but a way of thinking, and is reflective of the breakdown of centralized institutional authority. The idea of "We the people" goes far beyond politics, after all, evoking the principles of democracy that guide those societies that have a good degree of faith and trust in their citizens. For any organization, grassroots can function as a strategic platform that is likely to serve all parties—employees, clients, partners, and consumers—well in the future. Getting people involved at the local or basic level is an excellent means of building solid, enduring relationships—one of the cornerstones for long-term success.

Future Trend 27: Grassroots

Decision-Making and Leadership Platform

Implications

The concept of grassroots is spreading like a weed around the world.

- The dispersion of ideas and deconcentration of power is a very good thing.

The erosion of borders and the easy sharing of information and opinions are driving grassroots.

- Globalization and digitalization are advancing centuries-old democratic ideals.

Grassroots is rooted in politics but evident in many other areas of life.

- This is consistent with the rising tide of bottom-up over top-down ideologies.

It is in organizations' best interests to embrace grassroots thinking and action.

- It embodies the positives of transparency and customer-first corporate culture.

Grassroots-based causes will inform consumer attitudes and behavior.

- Passion points often guide brand choices.

Grassroots communities will cross social and economic boundaries of age, gender, race, class, and geography.

- It is potentially a better way to reach consumers than through traditional segmentation techniques.

Opportunities

Tap into the power of grassroots communities that complement your organization's mission.

- People want to be involved in endeavors in which they believe.

(*continued*)

Future Trend 27 (*continued*)

Adopt messaging platforms that resonate with members of large grassroots communities.

- Nonpartisan communications promote personal empowerment and respect for others.

Think global and act local.

- Express universal values on a customized geographic basis.

Invite consumers to be part of your organization's decision-making process.

- Trade upon the Founding Fathers' faith and trust in "We the people."

Encourage grassroots thinking in your corporate culture.

- Reward employees who approach their jobs as "activists."

Recognize that the future of business, like politics, is grassroots.

- "Brand populism" will become an important marketing strategy in the years ahead.

Future Trend 28: Disintegration

"The postwar geopolitical system is breaking down, and what comes next could be highly volatile—especially for big corporations," observed Chrystia Freeland in the *Atlantic* in 2015, thinking that this Future Trend pointed to nothing less than "the disintegration of the world." As suggested by Future Trend 21, geopolitics is an increasingly unstable affair, as our post–World War II roller coaster ride fueled by globalization and free markets spins more and more out of control. Radicalism from all sides of the political spectrum and economic inequality of massive proportions are just two factors contributing to this crumbling of the world order in place since the end of that war. Trust in large institutions, including Big Business, has dropped like a rock over the past few years, according to a recent survey by Edelman, a sign perhaps of even more fragmentation to come.[24]

Again, history helps to put things in perspective. In his 2016 book *Ages of Discord*, Peter Turchin found that great civilizations of the past went through cycles of integration and disintegration, making our current wave of geopolitical turmoil just part of the usual pattern of history. The Roman, Frankish, and German empires all experienced cycles of dramatic ups and downs, and China's political stability over the last couple of thousand years graphically appears like the electrocardiogram chart of a heart attack victim. Protracted periods of peace and broad prosperity are typically followed by eras defined by violence, terrorism, civil war, and other manifestations of social and economic dissonance, in other words, suggesting that today's global discord is, while disturbing, nothing really new.[25]

Which nations are most likely to disintegrate? Those with a large percentage of poor people, not surprisingly, with great inequalities along both income and gender lines also something likely to incite trouble. Corrupt governments and autocracy are other major contributors to a state's implosion, and youth—the less time a nation has existed—correlates with failure. Too many people and too little food are other factors in the collapse of a society, understandably, and suppression of human rights and religious freedom are strong negatives as well. The United States may appear to be resistant to disintegration based on these criteria presented by Charles W. Kegley and Shannon L. Blanton in their book *World Politics: Trend and Transformation*, but Turchin compares the current state of the nation to that of the 1850s—not exactly a vote of confidence for the future given what happened next.[26]

How does all this relate to how businesses should do business? Organizations large and small must recognize that they are not functioning in a vacuum, and are subject to events they cannot control. If we are indeed living in an age of discord, which seems difficult to argue, companies should proactively manage the chaotic geopolitical climate as best they can. Scenario planning is part of this, of course, as is gaining the larger understanding that it's in the best interests of any business to do the right thing on the local level. Furthering self-interests via hegemonic practices may have been an effective strategy during the Cold War years, but that no longer holds true. "As we grope our way toward a new domestic and international order, successful businesses will be the ones that recognize the truism that business and politics are inseparable," Freeland concluded, advising that organizations not just make contingency plans but invest in "the greater good wherever they operate."[27]

Future Trend 28: Disintegration

Decision-Making and Leadership Platform

Implications

Disintegration is likely to be a key theme of the future.

- The splintering of the political universe will accelerate.

The global scrambling for power is reminiscent of that of a century ago.

- Breakdown of the postwar, bipolar model is predicated on capitalism versus communism.

Largeness of all kinds will be increasingly viewed as a negative.

- It is no longer possible to be all things to all people because of rising polarization.

Business and politics are increasingly intertwined.

- Free-market capitalism is the connecting thread.

It is incumbent upon multinational organizations to determine how to thrive in an age of discord.

- Global turmoil and chaos is the new normal.

Knowledge of political goings-on is now part of management's responsibilities.

- It is a good time for Poli Sci majors.

Opportunities

Become fluent in the ever-evolving geopolitical landscape.

- Gain deep knowledge of present risk-intensive situations and likely future scenarios.

Treat disintegration as a long-term trend rather than as an anomaly.

- It is clear that we are in a historical cycle of discord.

Operate as a collection of small organizations versus one big one.

- Avert the declining trust in large institutions.

(continued)

Future Trend 28 (*continued*)

Embody traits of nation-state solidity within your own organization.

- These include economic and gender equality, honesty, democracy, commitment to human rights.

Structure your corporate culture around universally recognized values.

- These comprise community, family, the power of the individual.

Invest in "the greater good."

- Show sensitivity to local political and social climates.

Future Trend 29: Anti-politics

What's the most extreme example of citizens' dissatisfaction with the traditional political process? Anti-politics, naturally, or the rejection of party and electoral politics. Long before the kerfuffle over Donald Trump's brand of authoritarianism, many people have expressed their discontent with mainstream politics and how it shapes the economic and social landscape. Politics' breeding of American-style consumer capitalism is considered its worst offense to its many critics, with a host of social ills—war and environmental destruction, to name just two—labeled outgrowths of that malevolent ideology. It would be easy to dismiss such thinking as exclusive to a small group of radical extremists who want to overthrow the system for some kind of collectivist (or anarchic) society, but that would be overly simplistic. There is actually much to learn from the flourishing of global anti-politics, even for those who serve as its primary enemies.

In a nutshell, people who identify with the anti-politics movement recognize that mainstream politicians, whether Democratic or Republican, liberal or conservative, are in bed with the cultural and financial elite (and typically belong to that group themselves). While they claim to be for the people, the argument goes, such politicians are really for themselves and others like them (i.e., the rich and powerful who are solely interested in furthering their own agenda). Keeping the wheels of consumer capitalism turning is essentially that agenda, as doing so provides its relatively few leaders with copious rewards while at the same time treating the majority as mere pawns in the game. The game is thus rigged, proponents of anti-politics sensibly argue, reason enough for us to rethink who we elect and how we elect them.

Especially when applied to anti-politics, it's important to make a distinction between "politics" and "political." Those subscribing to anti-politics reject the mainstream, partisan political system, but are themselves highly political (i.e., interested in public affairs). Anti-politics is actually a highly political movement, and one that continues to attract more people around the world who are disenchanted with their respective established governments and leadership.[28] Not surprisingly, those considered to be outside the system are proving to be popular (and populist) candidates among those leaning toward anti-politics. Donald Trump (on the right) and Bernie Sanders (on the left) served as the most obvious examples of anti-politics in the 2016 presidential campaign, but many other countries are experiencing similar movements. Because it is so widespread and connected to related Future Trends, anti-politics is an important political phenomenon whose roots reside in past and present inequalities related to race, gender, and class.

Businesspeople should care about anti-politics, and not just because they are often cast as villains in the story. Like its cousins, Future Trends Populism, Rogueism, and Grassroots, Anti-politics serves as prime evidence that significant numbers of people around the world feel marginalized, disenfranchised, and largely powerless. Not just the underclass but much of the middle class feels this way, suggesting that there is something about anti-politics that goes far beyond envy or sour grapes. Citizens' anger and frustration that their governments are working against rather than for them, at least at the top levels, is an important consideration in terms of consumer insight. How can your organization empower consumers? managers should ask themselves, the answer possibly the key to a mutually beneficial relationship for many years.

Future Trend 29: Anti-politics

Decision-Making and Leadership Platform

Implications
Anti-politics is reflective of the growing discontent with large, powerful institutions.

- Multinational corporations are seen as a big part of the problem.

The anti-politics movement is not limited to radical extremists wishing to overthrow the government.

- There is broad-based sentiment that the elite are thwarting the promise of democracy.

(continued)

Future Trend 29 (*continued*)

It is critical that your organization is not perceived as part of or aligned with the ruling elite.

- "Insiders" are vulnerable to all kinds of criticism and attacks by those sympathetic to the anti-politics cause.

Political partisanship, regardless of slant, is especially dangerous.

- Politics—versus being political—is viewed as authoritarian and anti-democratic.

Citizens are not giving up hope that a more just and equal playing field can be created.

- They believe that good people and organizations can assume positions of leadership.

The celebration of materialism is an especially dangerous slope to go down.

- The values of friendship, sharing, and love are much more compelling.

Opportunities
Accommodate the concept of anti-politics in your organizational mission and vision.

- Fairness, honesty, and respect for the individual are at its core.

Weave democratic principles into all aspects of your company.

- Nurture the sense of belonging to something bigger and better than oneself.

Embed some level of outsider-ness into your corporate imaging.

- The establishment is increasingly viewed in negative terms.

Emphasize personal empowerment versus social status in advertising and promotion.

- Frame your product or service as an agent of confidence, contentment, and connectedness.

Ground your brands in communitarian (versus self-oriented) values.

- How does your product or service bring people together?

Demonstrate good corporate citizenship.

- Subscribe to ESG (environmental, social, governance) principles.

Future Trend 30: Green

Think green politics is a single-issue party solely dedicated to environmental-ism? Think again. While preventing pollution, promoting recycling, protest-ing overdevelopment, and tackling other environmental causes are indeed primary activities of the party, green politics is actually a bigger movement that addresses a wide range of related social and economic issues. Greenies believe that the system as a whole is really the problem, a conclusion that more people around the world are reaching. In a world of finite space and limited resources, green politics is going to eclipse centuries-old parties like the Democrats and the Republicans, I believe, as it represents a bigger, more universal idea: to save the earth from destruction. "The first rule of green politics is that you cannot divorce the economic system and human values from the health of the planet," wrote Peter Barnett in *Green World* (the of-ficial magazine of the Green Party), making it clear that the party supports "a radical program advocating a total transformation of the social, economic and political systems that currently prevail."[29]

As other Future Trends in the political arena make clear, partisanship is on the decline virtually everywhere, but the Green Party is an exception. The party benefits from drawing people of all political leanings, with the common denominator being the understanding that continual growth is a threat to not just the environment but humanity itself. A host of issues—health, crime, poverty, and many others—are seen as interdependent with what the party calls the politics of ecology, there being a symbiotic relation-ship between people and the planet. "Green Politics aims to reconstruct the patterns of human activities and relationships so that they come to respect and value the natural systems on which they depend," Barnett continued, the party determined to fight for its cause until "equity and social justice are woven into the fabric of society."[30]

Like other political movements, the Green Party is becoming more radi-cal, recognizing that this is the only way it will achieve its lofty goals. Cli-mate change has infused the organization with a sense of urgency, and served as a central rallying point. Capitalism runs on greenhouse gases, so taking on the "carbon economy" is one of the party's main initiatives. "Political dysfunction and economic dysfunction reinforce each other to drive eco-logical dysfunction," claimed Jedediah Purdy in the *Daily Beast*, of the belief that "only by thinking very big will we save the world." Only with a global effort can climate change be addressed, Purdy makes clear, as greenhouse gases spread throughout the atmosphere and do not care a whit from which country they originate. "We need a politics that crosses national borders and the borders between generations," he concluded, with Greenies ideally positioned to take on that role.[31]

As capitalists, for the most part, businesspeople have a responsibility to take the Green Party's message seriously, if only to have a deeper understanding of a trend that shows no signs of going away. People around the world recognize that there is an environmental cost to consumption, making it in the best interests of organizations to embrace the politics of ecology. Thinking and acting green is a virtually unbeatable hand, in fact, as it appeals to consumers of all social and economic backgrounds. As climate change and other environmental problems become more serious in the years and decades ahead, those organizations considered to be green will undoubtedly benefit greatly in terms of consumer loyalty, brand preference, and corporate goodwill. More importantly, it's the right thing to do.

Future Trend 30: Green

Decision-Making and Leadership Platform

Implications
Green is much more than the traditional notion of environmentalism.

- The politics of ecology is now recognized as interdependent with social and economic issues.

The concern about finite space and limited resources is intensifying.

- More people on the planet, growing middle classes, and spreading consumer culture is fueling green politics.

Climate change is serving as a lightning rod for green politics around the world.

- Consensus in the global scientific community is that it is real and dangerous.

Green is perhaps the only truly international and multicultural form of politics.

- Green is a language that anyone and everyone in the world can speak.

(continued)

Future Trend 30 (*continued*)

It is impossible to think of a more important goal than that of the Green Party.

- "Saving the planet" is the ultimate organizational mission statement.

Greenism and capitalism are not at all oppositional or mutually exclusive.

- They are entirely harmonious, complementary, and synergistic.

Opportunities
Go Green!

- Embed the politics of ecology throughout your organization.

Be a loud and proud voice of Greenism in your communications mix.

- It is one of the very few causes that resonates with global citizenship.

Use Green as a primary messaging platform to demonstrate your commitment to the cause.

- Serve as an example for other organizations to follow.

Partner with Green advocacy groups.

- These include the Sierra Club, World Wildlife Fund, the Nature Conservancy, Friends of the Earth; etc.

Support social and economic issues related to Green politics.

- They comprise social justice; grassroots democracy; human rights and freedom; global health, poverty, and hunger.

Champion Greenism in your local community.

- Reward employees for volunteering at the grassroots level.

CHAPTER FOUR

~

Social Trends

Economic and political trends may be the nuts and bolts of the future, but social trends function as the stuff that greases the wheels and makes the whole thing move. And more than the economy and politics (and technology, for that matter), the social arena reflects relationships between people and how we really live. Social trends often get lost in the sauce of futurism, overlooked by the race for money, the struggle for power, and our fascination with machines. A closer look, however, reveals that the ways in which societies operate serve as luminous beacons for the future and thus give important clues to how businesspeople should approach decision making and leadership for both the short and long term. Again, seemingly inconsistent forces are at work: trends such as omniculturalism and connectedness suggest that we are becoming more and more alike and that geography is virtually irrelevant, yet trends such as microfamilies, co-living, and localization indicate that personal relationships and having a sense of place is arguably more important than ever.

Much as other categories of trends, those revolving in the social sphere make it clear that change always serves as the primary currency of the future. Paradoxes and contradictions are nearly everywhere, something that is entirely consistent with the nature of shifting cultural plates. The tag teaming of diversity and commonality is a perfect example of how the world can be moving in two seemingly opposite directions at the same time. The quest for both humanistic values and technological advances is another dichotomy that demands unpacking, as is the curious dynamic between globalization and localization. As well, people in emerging societies are gravitating toward materialistic values while those in more developed ones are drifting toward a belief set grounded in post-materialism—this too is worth pondering.

Alongside such enigmatic, bidirectional forces are developments that leave little doubt what the world will be like for the foreseeable future. We are becoming not just more interconnected but blended, for example, a function of our ever-shrinking planet and ever-growing global economy. Families are becoming smaller as women make significant strides in the workplace and as gender roles become more fluid. As Future Trend 15 made clear, the middle-classing in much of the world is one of the great stories of our time and place, and perhaps serves as the biggest opportunity for organizations to grow. As well, cities are getting larger as hundreds of millions of people with income levels below the middle class compete in the global economy. While managing such cultural change is challenging to say the least, particularly against the backdrop of some of the more worrisome Future Trends discussed in chapters 2 and 3, businesspeople have a historic chance to expand into new markets and achieve whatever goals they set.

Finally, good old demography is playing a large role in shaping the future. The world's population is aging, we all know, with the ways in which baby boomers decide to spend the third act of their lives to serve as a major chunk of the framework of society over the next couple of decades. The reality that many more millions of older people will soon be occupying the planet is making some experts predict that the sky will soon be falling, a scenario with which I disagree. Millennials and post-millennials, meanwhile, are changing the rules of the game just as younger generations always do, in their case by infusing both their personal and professional lives with an extra-heavy dose of socialization. If there's any reason to dismiss the notion that a generational war is on the horizon as boomers and millennials fight over resources, it's that each huge group is deeply committed to contributing or giving back to society in some way. This will serve as a key unifying force in the years ahead, I believe, some very good news as we move forward into the world of tomorrow.

Future Trend 31: Omniculturalism

What is "the unstoppable global trend," according to Mike Fromowitz, writing for campaignasia.com? Multiculturalism, or the presence of different racial and ethnic groups within a society. More countries are becoming more multicultural as people move about in greater numbers than ever before, a Future Trend that shows no signs of reversing. I prefer to call this force omniculturalism, or the increasing cultural diversity of nations, regions, and local communities. The number of international migrants is in the hundreds of millions—no one knows exactly how many—dramatically raising the number of those foreign born in many cities around the world. Higher birth rates among minority groups are the other main factor driving omniculturalism. In the United States, the percentage of white people has dropped over the past decade, while the number of African Americans has risen by 22 percent, Hispanic Americans by 58 percent, and Asian Americans by 72 percent.[1] Whites will become the minority here in 2043, the US Census predicts, and other countries are experiencing similar shifting of their respective demographic plates.[2]

But some experts in demography believe the United States, and by implication other nations because of their own population makeups, are already transcultural. EthniFacts, a research and marketing firm, is leading the way in such thinking, an approach that challenges the overly simplistic "majority" vis-à-vis "minority" paradigm. EthniFacts rejects the notion that there is a white "mainstream" and various racial and ethnic groups that fall outside of it; the company makes a convincing case that we really are now in many ways the melting pot social scientists of decades past proposed we were. Rather than the individual-based data the Census Bureau relies on, we should view our cultural identity in social terms (i.e., how we are living multiethnic lives in relation to each other), regardless of our personal ethnic identity. Anyone living in any major city experiences omniculturalism daily, after all, with all the stuff that goes into defining culture—language, food, the arts, and much more—a truer measure of society and its people than each individual's ancestral background. America reached a tipping point in 2013 when most of the country became multicultural as measured in their terms, EthniFacts claimed, an interesting idea that poses major implications for how we think about our national and even personal identities.[3]

If one buys into this theory, which I do, it's incumbent upon business-people to replace the tired majority-minority trope with one that more accurately reflects the idea that most if not all of us are already effectively transcultural. "The New Mainstream," EthniFacts posits, is "an America Reimagined where the 'general market' no longer exists, but rather a market-place that reflects and acknowledges consumers of all races and ethnicities as the source of new social trends and business growth and demands activation strategies based on this reality."[4] Instead of dividing the American pie into neat slices defined by an individual's race or ethnicity, in other words, marketers might work from the supposition that we are a transcultural society and will become more of one in the future. Such an approach is superior to the slice-and-dice model, I believe; we are, more than anything else, social organisms who consume all kinds of cultural experiences. In fact, one could make a solid case that America has always been a transcultural nation, this the thing that has made us distinct from all others. As the world becomes increasingly transcultural, organizations have the opportunity to talk to consumers in a new and different way, an exciting proposition.

Future Trend 31: Omniculturalism

Decision-Making and Leadership Platform

Implications

America and most of the rest of the world are becoming more omnicultural.

- Cultural commonality is arguably the most significant Future Trend over the long term.

The concept of multiculturalism within the business arena is tired.

- Companies have been breaking down the marketplace by race, ethnicity, and nationality since the Eisenhower administration.

Many biases are built into a majority-minority view of society.

- That view assumes that white people are the mainstream and the norm.

Multiculturalism is also limited through its tendency to silo populations.

- It is not reflective of how people actually interact in pluralistic societies.

Omniculturalism is a more interesting and insightful way to view society and consumers.

- It directly acknowledges that we are all woven into a patchwork quilt of people and cultures.

Omniculturalism is entirely consistent with accelerating globalization.

- The earth as a whole is, as it was said decades ago, becoming a giant melting pot.

Opportunities

Embrace the omniculturalism concept.

- View the marketplace in transcultural versus multicultural terms.

Reimagine America as a transcultural society.

- Resist sorting the population based on shade of skin or another external measure.

(continued)

Future Trend 31 (*continued*)

Assume that all consumers work and play in a transcultural world.

- Demographic divisions such as race and ethnicity (as well as gender, age, and ability) are increasingly irrelevant and misdirected.

Readopt the melting pot model.

- The "tossed salad" model is not receptive to how the ingredients of a society combine to form new flavors.

Treat each consumer as somehow transcultural.

- Most people are interested in exploring different dimensions of the human experience.

Trade on the fact that many individuals are biologically transcultural.

- DNA testing is revealing that most of us are a mixture of races and ethnicities.

Future Trend 32: Microfamilies

Like the world itself, metaphorically speaking, the global family is shrinking. "The family of the future is growing smaller in size with the average number of children per household dropping across regions, in both developed and emerging economies," noted Euromonitor International a few years back, citing dropping rates of fertility, more women in the workplace, couples waiting longer to have kids, and economic factors as reasons for smaller families worldwide. There will be just one child per household in 2020, according to that market research firm, which is about half the number there were in 1980. Relatedly, single-person and childless households have risen sharply over this same period, with almost twice as many of each as there were forty years ago.[5]

This radical transformation of family life within a relatively short period carries enormous social freight, especially for businesses. While households will be smaller, meaning fewer potential consumers, they will have more discretionary money and spend more of it on a per-person basis—a major driver of economic growth. More families will be able to own a car—good news for the automobile industry, obviously—and parents will be more likely to be able to send their children to college, a positive development for educators. Marketers should be especially excited about the increase in the number of single-person households; it is this consumer segment that spends the most for nonessential products and services such as appliances, mobile devices, computers, and entertainment.[6] Businesses offering products or services for children, on the other hand, should be concerned about a shrinking market.

What accounts for what is the most dramatic shift in family size since the advent of modern birth control a century ago? Globalization, for one thing, as economic mobility and Western-style social attitudes and behavior, including those toward family dynamics, increasingly permeate Asia, Latin America, and Africa. (See Future Trend 15, Middle-Classing.) The very Western idea of individualism is another major reason for the reduction of family size, with more people around the world apparently seeking more control over their personal and professional lives. As well, the simple inability for couples to afford to raise children is playing a big part in the increased number of smaller households; slow economic growth and high rates of unemployment in many parts of the world are clearly having a direct effect on family planning.[7]

Americans are part of this Future Trend toward smaller families. When Gallup asked Americans in 2013 what they thought was the ideal number of children for a family to have, almost half said two, a lower number than in past decades. The expense of bringing up a child was the most important reason for not having a child, something not surprising given what it costs to raise one. (Better have a quarter of a million bucks handy if you're considering becoming a parent, according to Department of Agriculture figures.) As well, mothers are far more likely to be working than a generation or two ago, another factor in more Americans' desire to have smaller families. Reality is reflecting these socioeconomic considerations; three times as many women became mothers to at least four children in 1976 than in 2014, the Pew Research Center reported, a function in large part of the gains made from second-wave feminism.[8] Look for the configuration of families to continue to be redefined both here and abroad due to ever-shifting social and economic gears.

Future Trend 32: Microfamilies

Decision-Making and Leadership Platform

Implications
The average family size is getting smaller on a global basis.

- This trend is a function of long-term social and economic factors.

Microfamilies are directly related to the rising global middle class.

- Many women are prioritizing careers and making money over having large families.

(continued)

Future Trend 32 (*continued*)

The desire for greater independence and autonomy is playing a greater role in the family planning process.

- It is a tricky balancing act between achieving one's personal goals and dedicating oneself to others.

The emergence of more fluid gender roles is another part of the equation.

- There is greater permission for women to be the breadwinner of their family.

Microfamilies are good news and bad news for most marketers.

- There will be fewer consumers, but with higher household discretionary spending power.

It is in the best interests of marketers to children to shift the product mix.

- There is little opportunity for growth in a declining segment.

Opportunities
Adapt your organization to the reality of smaller families.

- Lean more heavily toward adults and away from kids in marketing efforts.

Go after increasing discretionary spending power in developing nations.

- This is a big—perhaps the biggest—growth opportunity in business.

Develop new and innovative products and services that cater to the wants and needs of the smaller family.

- Provide more emphasis on quality versus quantity.

Flaunt Western-oriented values in the marketing communications platform.

- Family management is heavily steeped in postindustrial thinking and practice.

Feature ideas of independence and self-empowerment in advertising and corporate messaging.

- This is the underlying psychological basis of the decision to limit family size.

Trade on principles of feminist theory.

- Many women are freed from the patriarchal system that cast them in domestic roles.

Future Trend 33: Urbanization

In 1950, Urban Hub notes, 30 percent of people on this planet lived in cities; a century later, 70 percent of earthlings will reside in urban environments, an incredible transformation of our geographic and cultural landscape. Right now, more than 50 percent of people call cities home, something no previous generation could claim. Much of the urbanization over the next couple of decades will take place in developing nations in Asia, Latin America, the Middle East, and Africa, as more people move to cities for better housing, schools, health care, and cultural offerings. With no exaggeration, this mass migration is one of the most important developments in the history of our species, and something that presents major consequences in terms of how organizations should chart their own future.[9]

As with most Future Trends, there are positives and negatives associated with Urbanization. Most urbanites have a greater chance to prosper economically than rural folk, and the quality of life in cities is indeed often superior in many ways to that in small villages. Large numbers of people moving into a limited space creates a host of problems, however, making it likely that the years ahead will be busy ones for urban planners and others dealing with the infrastructure of cities. Making essential services such as sewage, electricity, and water run efficiently is in itself a huge proposition, and managing the transportation system of any major city is another daunting challenge. Designing sufficient space for tens of millions of people to live, work, and shop is probably the most critical task, the reason that "vertical cities" (thousands of people residing in tremendously tall buildings) are taking the architectural world by storm.[10]

As large cities expand not just upward but outward, they are increasingly bumping into each other, creating what are known as "megacities." By 2023, according to Frost & Sullivan, there will be thirty such jumbo metropolises, with these cities certain to experience high economic growth. And when two or more nearby megacities start to converge, the result is a megaregion, a massive area with populations exceeding those of many countries. Johannesburg and Pretoria in South Africa, for example, are two such megacities smashing into each other, with that region becoming known as "Jo-Toria." If that were not enough, surging urbanization is also responsible for megacorridors, or passageways that connect megacities or regions and themselves contain huge populations. One hundred twenty million people will be living in the Hong Kong–Shenzhen-Guangzhou corridor in China by 2025, the research company predicts, just one of many fast-growing urban strips around the world.[11]

While again, managing megaurban environments presents immense challenges, many businesses are well positioned to capitalize on the emergence of more large cities. "The explosive population growth and dynamic shift in urban sprawl, coupled with the economic growth of megacities in the emerging economies, will pose a variety of opportunities for companies operating in different sectors," states Frost & Sullivan, believing that "the megacities from the emerging economies will become the largest markets for existing premium products and technologies." Cities such as Sao Paolo, Buenos Aires, Delhi, Mumbai, Beijing, Shanghai, and Moscow will thus be where much of the action will be in the future, suggesting that more globally oriented organizations shift their assets and resources from North America and Europe to South America and Asia.[12]

Future Trend 33: Urbanization

Decision-Making and Leadership Platform

Implications

The thousands-of-years-long trend toward urbanization is accelerating.

- There is a natural human urge for people to congregate.

There is no substitute for resources and assets found only in the real world.

- Certain things are impossible to replicate in the online universe.

Urbanization is running parallel with the middle-classing of emerging countries.

- It is directly connected to the desire to compete in the global economy and achieve upward mobility.

Making large cities work is one of the greatest challenges of the twenty-first century.

- There are all kinds of issues to address when more than ten million people decide to live in the same place.

All aspects of sustainability are vital to the development of megacities.

- Vision: connected, inclusive, and environmentally friendly communities.

(continued)

Future Trend 33 (*continued*)

"Smartness" is also key.

- Urbanization requires economic, technological, and governance smartness.

Opportunities
Capitalize on the megatrend of urbanization.

- What can your organization contribute to the enormous needs of megacities, regions, and corridors?

Focus organizational resources on South America and Asia.

- The highest growth opportunities are in these continents as millions of people move to cities.

Work outward from basic services.

- Utilities, transportation, housing, etc., are key to urbanization.

Trade on successful models of urban planning and infrastructure.

- Emulate cities that incorporate dimensions of sustainability and smartness.

View cities as urban ecosystems.

- They are living, breathing organisms that require considerable attention to survive and thrive.

Forge partnerships between the private and public sectors.

- Alliances between businesses and local governments are essential.

Future Trend 34: Co-Living

"Trend alert! Communes are back!" declares Molly Wood of marketplace. org, then making it clear that we shouldn't start filling our closets with tie-dyed shirts and love beads. But much like forty years ago, group housing or co-living is popular with 20- and 30somethings who are similarly attracted to the ideas of community, sharing costs and housework, and round-the-clock socializing opportunities. Just as many of that demographic are choosing to gather in co-working spaces in their professional lives, so are they turning their personal lives into a group affair. A myriad of start-ups all over the world such as Open Door, Common, Pure House, WeLive, Roam, Podshare, Zoku, and Lyf are rushing into co-living, recognizing that it presents a poten- tially highly profitable business model.[13]

Why are birds of a feather (often technogeeks, creative types, and students) flocking together? Co-living is a prime example of millennials' desire for independence, and preference not to be be tied down by owning a property and having a mortgage. (College debt—the scourge of that gen- eration—makes that impossible for many regardless of preferences.) Young people are getting married later in life than ever before, another reason to hook up with others in a group housing setting. "This suspended adulthood and the rise of the digital nomad result in an increase in mobility and a reduced desire to settle," explains James Scott, CEO of the Collective, one of the growing number of companies offering co-living services.[14] The Col- lective recently opened Old Oak in London, which offers its 500+ lucky residents not just posh flats but a game room, mini-movie theater, library, and spa.[15] Sign me up!

Deeper cultural forces are in play, however, suggesting a bright future for co-living in all kinds of configurations. The broader culture shift in postindustrial societies toward acquiring experiences versus possessions, for example, is pushing more people to opt not to buy a home and all the stuff that has to go into it. If Uber makes owning a car unnecessary and Netflix means not having to have cable, it can be argued that co-living liberates people from deeper debt. Urban isolation is another contributing factor for the rise of co-living, as many paradoxically feel more alone in a large city.[16] And for those for whom social media is not a fun diversion but a way of life, what makes more sense than a socially oriented living arrangement in which one can share more life moments with others?[17]

With maid service and "instant friends" in a "ready-made" community, it's not surprising that those with the financial resources (often a couple grand or more per month) are choosing to co-live. A dozen or perhaps many more people might live in this new, more upscale, and branded version of "hacker houses" (the dwellings in which many tech entrepreneurs in the Bay Area, including Mark Zuckerberg and some Facebook pals, collectively crashed during and after the dot-com bubble). At its best, co-living provides its resi- dents with a strong sense of togetherness, with some group houses offering, shades of the Summer of Love, community gardens and nightly jam sessions. Other co-living formats are designed around plush furnished apartments for young people starting out with a new job in a new city.[18] Whatever the for- mat, co-living is a promising alternative to the private, sometimes insulated living spaces most of us inhabit. "Essentially, it is a small town under one roof, but with better amenities, where you actually get to know your neigh- bours," says Lucy Ingham of factor-tech.com, "a pretty appealing prospect."[19]

Future Trend 34: Co-Living

Decision-Making and Leadership Platform

Implications

More people are choosing to live together in group settings.

- Co-living makes sense for all kinds of reasons.

Many different expressions of "groupness" are on the rise.

- Co-living is the flip side of millennials' attraction to shared work-spaces.

The freelance economy and co-living share a symbiotic relationship.

- Community is an essential part of the human experience.

A better name for millennials: "Generation S," for Socialization.

- Socialization (i.e., sharing one's life with others), is at the heart of the group's individual and collective identity.

Co-living is reflective of 20- and 30-somethings' natural inclination to rewrite social norms.

- It is consistent with their historic delay in getting married, having kids, and owning homes.

Contemporary young adults are hardwired to rent versus own in all aspects of life.

- The generation is putting freedom, independence, and flexibility in front of materialistically defined social status.

Opportunities

Latch onto millennials' leanings toward communal experiences.

- The generation of social media natives are innately oriented to think and act socially in all aspects of life.

Look for other opportunities to communalize and socialize young adults' lives.

- How can each moment be transformed from an individual to group experience?

(*continued*)

Future Trend 34 (*continued*)

Create products and services steeped in youthful rootlessness and rest-lessness.

- Adopt a rent versus own model of consumerism.

Redefine brand deliverables from possessive to experiential terms.

- See your organization's offering as verbs versus nouns.

Target co-living communities to reach innovative, ahead-of-the-curve consumers.

- They are "influencers" who can potentially shape mainstream sentiment toward a product category or brand.

Revisit other modern interpretations of countercultural phenomena.

- Many millennials are drawn to 1960s-style communitarianism.

Future Trend 35: Graying

"Global aging will become the transcendent political and economic issue of the twenty-first century," wrote Peter G. Peterson back in 1999 in his book *Gray Dawn*, ringing an alarm bell about the demographic iceberg that lay dead ahead in the world's path. As the baby boomer population reached its senior years, the billionaire businessman warned, the nation's economy and healthcare system would each crash, unable to support and meet the needs of that many older people.[20] A good number of economists today agree with Peterson, with some pundits predicting a generational war to be fought between boomers and millennials over taxpayer resources.

While this apocalyptic scenario is open to debate (I think the aging of boomers will actually help the economy and society at large by creating millions of much-needed jobs), there is no doubt that the aging of what was the largest generation in history (until the millennials came around) will have a profound social, economic, and political impact on America and much of the world. Indeed, a solid case can be made that the age wave is the most significant socioeconomic trend in the United States today, as sixty-five million (of the original seventy-six million) boomers (who in 2017 range in age from fifty-three to seventy-one) head into their senior years *en masse*. Ten thousand boomers are turning sixty-five every day, an unprecedented demographic tsunami. In 2029, the year when the last boomer will have turned sixty-five, there will still be over sixty-one million boomers, according to the Census Bureau, about 17.2 percent of the projected population of the United States.[21]

The aging of America and the world also presents major implications for businesses in virtually all industries and product categories. Boomers are still the key to the marketplace despite marketers' obsession with youth, due in part to their collective wealth and propensity to consume. As a group, boomers are going to have the highest net worth in the United States until at least 2030, according to the Deloitte Center for Financial Services, with their portion of total assets less liabilities to reach a high of 50 percent by 2020. By 2030, boomers' net household wealth is forecast to be 44.5 percent, still an impressive number that marketers will have to consider when choosing whom to target with products and services.[22]

Likewise, boomers' buyer power is and will remain huge. While boomers represent about a quarter of the nation's population, they currently hold 70 percent of disposable income, according to a report by Nielsen and BoomAgers. Boomers are buying about half of total consumer-packaged goods (CPG) and dominate purchases in 119 of 123 CPG categories, more reasons that marketers should not think the group's best consumer days are behind them.[23] As well, widely held stereotypes of older consumers are just untrue. Most companies no doubt want to market to boomers because of their discretionary dollars and sheer numbers, but now may no longer know how to, thinking perhaps that older consumers are interested only in products and services for the aged. Research shows that most boomers are not interested in radically downsizing, however, and are as open as ever to new brand experiences. As "professional" consumers their whole lives, boomers will keep spending money until they go off to the big Woodstock in the sky, making it a mistake for marketers to ignore them in their later years. As I detailed in my book *Boomers 3.0*, creating meaningful relationships with baby boomers in their third act of life should be a priority for all kinds of businesses, something that demands a new kind of thinking and an alternative set of tools.[24]

Future Trend 35: Graying

Decision-Making and Leadership Platform

Implications

There are good reasons for having major concerns about global aging.

- Graying is an unprecedented demographic event requiring major policy changes.

There is no compelling evidence yet of an economic and healthcare meltdown, however.

- Fears are reminiscent of apocalyptic predictions concerning over-population in the early 1970s.

Baby boomers are not ready to go silently into the night.

- Their third act of life (two or three more decades) is still to come.

Business opportunities of an aging population are going largely ignored.

- Youth-obsessed marketers are overlooking a very large, very wealthy group of consumers.

Commonly held beliefs about older consumers are unfounded.

- Research shows that 60- and 70somethings are receptive to new products and services.

Different strategies are required, however, to effectively market to baby boomers.

- The third act of life is very different from the first and second.

Opportunities

Speak to baby boomers as if they were still young (at heart).

- Tell older people that youth is about what one does and how one feels versus how one looks.

Leverage older dogs' wish to learn new tricks in their third act.

- Don't underestimate boomers' desire to learn new things.

(continued)

Future Trend 35 (*continued*)

Think of older people as a work in process open to new experiences.

- Plug into boomers' passions when marketing to them.

Offer older people ways of wisdom as its cultural currency increases.

- Define your brand as an opportunity for boomers to realize self-actualization.

Invest in the "grandparent economy" as more boomers join its ranks.

- The number of grandparents is at a historic high and still growing.

Make an AARP partnership a staple of your marketing efforts to boomers.

- There are good reasons to take sides with the loudest champion of anti-agism.

Future Trend 36: Causes

The measure of a person's life is the affect they have on others.

—Ex-professional basketball player Steve Nash

What's a good way for a person to become less depressed, have lower blood pressure, and live longer? Give money and/or time to a cause in which he or she believes. Many studies show that giving and volunteering are good for one's health, as being generous is an important source of happiness for those who choose to do it. Givers are not just happier and healthier than non-givers but also have a stronger sense of purpose and higher self-esteem, more reason to be excited about the philanthropic windfall that is looming. It turns out that helping people in need offers a greater opportunity to find joy in life than spending money on oneself, something that perhaps should make all of us question our priorities.[25]

Many millennials are deeply committed to the causes in which they believe, suggesting that advocacy and action will play a significant role in our collective future. It is, however, baby boomers who will most powerfully shape philanthropy over the next quarter-century; it is again that generation that accounts for the largest percentage of financial resources and is naturally inclined to give back in some way. The graying of the world is thus directly connected to the increasing value of creating positive social change, perhaps the most upbeat Future Trend of all. As well, creating some form of legacy is top of mind for many boomers, as more and more ask themselves, "How can or will I be remembered?"[26]

In fact, it is difficult to overestimate baby boomers' interest in making others know that they spent some time on earth, in the process realizing a legitimate form of immortality. Needless to say, this is a highly valuable pursuit, and a genuine way to effectively extend one's life span or live forever (versus the false promise of "anti-aging"). Upwards of 90 percent of Americans aged sixty-five or older currently give in some way, making many nonprofit causes giddy with excitement because of the number of boomers. Boomers already contribute about 43 percent of all dollars given in the United States, a study by the software firm Blackbaud found, the highest percentage of any generation to date.[27]

Whether younger or older, people have two primary ways to contribute to causes: money and time. While millennials reach their peak earning years over the next couple of decades, it is undoubtedly baby boomers who will do the philanthropic heavy lifting. Boomers are expected to donate $8 trillion to charities over the following twenty years in either money or time as volunteers, according to a 2015 study conducted by Merrill Lynch, a transfer of wealth that will reshape the philanthropic landscape of the country and world. "Boomers are famous for wanting to do things their own way and change the world, and charitable giving will be the next chapter in their impact," wrote Allison Pond in the *Deseret News*, with most "wanting to be more personally involved in the causes they care about."[28] Making real, measurable change is the goal, replacing the previous model of charity in which complete trust was placed with nonprofits to spend money as they saw fit. Boomers tend to "invest" in a charity rather than just give it away, seeing their contribution as "philanthropic venture capital." More than anything else, individual passions will drive boomer philanthropy—valuable fodder for many organizations to consider when reaching out to them in the future.[29]

Future Trend 36: Causes

Decision-Making and Leadership Platform

Implications
Causes of all kinds are rising in intensity and commitment.

- "Postmaterialist" societies typically devote energy and resources toward creating positive change.

(continued)

Future Trend 36 (*continued*)

The desire to advance beliefs and ideals is a powerful motivator for behavior.

- Ultimate goal: to create a better world, however defined.

Causes are a win-win phenomenon for both giver and givee.

- This is humanity at its best.

The next two decades will be a golden age for philanthropy.

- The wealthiest generation in history is ready to share their literal good fortune.

Millennials too are playing a principal role in creating a more altruistic society.

- Empathy and idealism are a natural part of a younger generation's DNA.

A different kind of philanthropy is now in play.

- Giving is perceived as a kind of business decision requiring personal attention versus simply writing a check.

Opportunities
Build causes into your organization's DNA.

- Offer innovative ways for consumers to get involved in worthy endeavors such as teaching and mentoring.

Plan now for the biggest transfer of wealth in history.

- An estimated $30 trillion is on the table.

Champion corporate volunteering.

- Reward employees for giving some of their time to a relevant cause.

Win consumer loyalty by building in philanthropic causes to your brands' deliverables.

- Causes are a primary source of added value.

(*continued*)

Future Trend 36 (*continued*)

Pitch baby boomers the ultimate pitch: a legacy.

- Create foundations, trusts, philanthropies, and nonprofits that some-how relate to your organization's mission and vision.

View consumers' involvement in causes as an alternative form of venture capital.

- This type of investment is just as valuable as money, if not more so.

Future Trend 37: Feminization

"This is the century of the woman," declared United Nations Deputy Sec-retary General Michelle Bachelet in 2014 at the "Women and Girls Rising" conference, making the case that it would be females who would lead the way in the future. Men had dominated human civilization since the begin-ning of history, Bachelet (who also happened to be president of Chile) pointed out, but the time was now right for a major turning of the gender tables. The twenty-first century would be the time in which women would finally achieve equal rights around the world, a victory allowing them to realize their full potential. While much progress along these lines had been made, there was still a long way to go; significant gender gaps remained in education, the workplace, government, and basic human rights, a function of persistent and oppressive expressions of masculinity. "We must seize every opportunity, at all levels, to realize women's and girls' human rights and full and equal participation in society," Bachelet told her audience; the larger result would be a more peaceful and just world.[30]

In truth, for more than a century now, much of the world has become increasingly feminized (i.e., imbued with female-oriented traits or character-istics). For decades, in fact, one's "emotional intelligence" has risen in value as social currency, with the defining attributes of the alpha male (e.g., aggres-sion, competitiveness, risky behavior, and physicality) less and less in favor. Speaking in general terms, of course, women have a different way of seeing the world and an alternative approach to decision making and leadership than that of men. Going further, it is a more feminine outlook or mindset that appears to be more in synch with the way that the world is headed and with the measures by which we will likely define achievement and accom-plishment. Testosterone, to put it more bluntly, is not the ideal asset to possess if one is intent on building collaborative communities and mutually beneficial partnerships—each of those to assuredly function as a main road to success in the future. The facts bear this out; study after study shows that performance in organizations improves when women are full participants, making it not surprising for those in the prediction business to conclude that "the future is female."[31]

The Future Trend of Feminization is especially salient for businesspeople interested in reaching more than half of the world's population. As previously discussed, more women are entering the global workforce, something that is certain to reshuffle the world's economic deck. Some have labeled this development as the birth of the "she-conomy" (i.e., a global economic system populated by greater numbers of urban, educated, technology-equipped, and affluent women). "In the industrialized world, women will continue making educational, economic and political advances," forecasts intuit.com,with "the gender gap in earnings to approach parity by 2020."[32] It is again the non-industrialized world where the real growth will take place, however, with more than 90 percent of first-time female workers to come from developing nations.[33]

The prospect of almost a billion more women possessing discretionary income is reason enough to rethink the very parameters of consumerism. Capacity for growth will be defined not just by geography (i.e., having a presence in the developing world) but along gender lines as well. Females will have significantly greater influence in purchasing behavior, a progressive step that is long overdue and one that is entirely consistent with our more feminized world of the future.

Future Trend 37: Feminization

Decision-Making and Leadership Platform

Implications
The world is becoming increasingly feminine, less masculine.

- Feminization has much to do with the middle-classing of developing countries.

There is greater recognition and value of women in the global workforce.

- This is taking place forty or so years after the Western feminist movement led to (theoretical) gender equality.

(continued)

Future Trend 37 (*continued*)

The time is right for the ascendance of women.

- A female perspective and personality is more consistent with contemporary social values.

Feminization is running parallel with globalization.

- Changes in gender dynamics are creating a more omnicultural world.

Gains made by women are a good thing on all levels.

- The best societies and organizations are receptive to complementary thinking and skills.

The global economy is evolving into more of a she-conomy.

- There are hundreds of millions more middle-class women in the pipeline.

Opportunities

Feminize your organization and brands.

- Embrace female-oriented values as they rise in worth.

Target middle-class women in developing nations.

- The bullseye is the "she-conomy."

Champion women's rights for full social and economic equality.

- This is a major moment in human history in terms of gender.

Partner with leading women's and girls' organizations in female-oriented initiatives.

- These include the National Organization for Women, National Women's Business Council, Girls Inc., etc.

Offer scholarships to young women from countries in which gender-based discrimination is pervasive.

- Reach out to big donors interested in education and women's rights.

Appoint exceptional young women as corporate ambassadors.

- Successful 20somethings can serve as role models for aspiring girls around the world.

Future Trend 38: Connectedness

"Coming Soon: Human Banking," reads a sign for TD Bank in my neighborhood, not just a clever ad but one that addresses the sad reality that interaction with real people is becoming a novelty. Technology is no doubt amazing and even magical by allowing us to do things that would be difficult or impossible just one generation ago. (Remember having to scrounge around for a quarter and then find a pay phone to call someone up to the late 1990s?) Shopping, which used to be an opportunity to bump into and catch up with neighbors, is a prime example. Having just about anything delivered right to your doorstop in a couple of days after trolling Amazon or thousands of other websites is nothing short of incredible from a historic perspective, as until the mid-nineteenth century or so it would require a European or American to spend months or years on a ship to score say, a pineapple. E-banking, e-learning, and e-everything else are similarly remarkable, saving us time and energy by staying in one spot and doing them all online.

The conquering of time and space will only escalate as the march of technology speeds up to a dash though automation and the creation of alternative universes. Through greater connectivity, the many technology gurus out there happily proclaim, our lives will become simpler and more convenient, leaving us more time to do, well, whatever. Already many of us no longer work in the same physical space as our coworkers, with the army of digital nomads to become exponentially larger with the emergence of the freelance economy. Like shopping, it strangely needs to be pointed out, work has traditionally served as a primary way for people to interact and form meaningful relationships that go beyond that possible through e-mail or even web-based conferencing.[34]

Are we really more connected as the geeks say we are, one has to ask? I'm not so sure, and nor is Dan Fennessy, founder of Amsterdam-based partywith-alocal.com. "There's a time coming (soon) when many of us won't actually have to see or speak to any other humans in real-life," Fennessey wrote in 2017 for medium.com, like me having decidedly mixed feelings about the side effects of our expanding digital universe. "A future with amazing, convenient and autonomous technology, but lacking in real life human connections, sounds pretty sad and lonely to me," he continues, citing research showing that we're not far away from such a scary scenario. Almost two out of every five millennials spend more time on their smart devices than with their friends, family members, or coworkers, according to a 2016 Bank of America study, a figure supporting my long-held belief that "social networks" actually tend to make us less social (precisely the reason you won't find me Facebooking, Pinteresting, Instagraming, Flickring, Tumblring, or Redditing).[35]

What will be our response to ever-expanding, often dehumanizing digitalization? Connectedness, I believe, a backlash to technological connectivity that promises to reaffirm the fact that we are, more than anything else, social animals who require real relationships to be happy, content people. "The best experiences in life are shared with family, friends, and like-minded people, in real life," Fennessey concluded, convincingly arguing that "human connection is part of what makes us human."[36] At its best, the Internet is an enabler of getting people together in real time and real space, making connectedness just as vital as connectivity in our collective future.

Future Trend 38: Connectedness

Decision-Making and Leadership Platform

Implications
Rising connectivity is leaving many of us longing for connectedness.

- There is no substitute for real (versus screen-based) relationships.

Connectivity will increase dramatically as the "Internet of Things" rolls on.

- Machines are destined to interact with each other.

Social networks are more about quantity than quality.

- They are a good way to keep in touch on a superficial basis with a large number of people.

Connectedness, like Future Trend 20 (Analogism), is a natural response to overwhelming digitality.

- There is a yearning for the physical yin to complement the non-physical yang.

There is a greater understanding that virtuality and reality are ideally complementary forces.

- E-tailers are increasingly incorporating bricks-and-mortar retail into their business models.

Connectedness is an enduring human value that transcends here-today, gone-tomorrow technology.

- Real relationships are more powerful than any device can possibly be.

(*continued*)

Future Trend 38 (*continued*)

Opportunities
Reinsert humanness throughout your organization.

- Remember that technology is just a tool to facilitate actual relationships.

Capitalize on consumers' need for connectedness.

- How can your organization get people together in the real world?

Ground your brands in measurable time and recognizable space.

- The online universe defies the natural laws of physics.

Put the "social" into social networks.

- Allow the opportunity for consumers with shared passions to meet at corporate-sponsored or -endorsed events.

Create products and services that act as catalysts for families and friends to get together.

- Gatherings with loved ones are often the most memorable experiences in life.

Adopt connectedness as a corporate or brand image.

- It is a hard-to-beat competitive position.

Future Trend 39: ESG

How are more people around the world making a positive and lasting social impact? Through Environmental, Social, and Governance (ESG) investing. Choosing to invest in companies that are doing good things and avoiding those that are not is quite literally putting one's money where one's mouth is. ESG (or "mission-driven") investment entails financial support of nonprofit organizations, companies that are socially responsible, and businesses managed by entrepreneurs with a social conscience. A growing number of people want their investments to match their values, sparking the growth of socially screened mutual funds. Rather than just one-offs, ESG investing is being increasingly packaged into funds such as the Bay Area Equity Fund managed by J. P. Morgan, which strives to realize average yields while at the same time creating employment opportunities in lower-income areas.[37]

ESG investments exemplify the transition from "socially responsible investing" (SRI), which has long been an attractive option for those not wanting to support "bad" corporations based on certain criteria. SRI usually excluded "sin industries" such as tobacco, alcohol, gambling, and military hardware, as well as environmentally insensitive companies. ESG, on the other hand, prioritizes selectivity over avoidance in portfolio design. Rather than eliminating certain industries or companies, ESG investing is based on choosing organizations that consistently enforce corporate governance, are environmentally friendly, or confront significant social issues. Corporate governance involves being transparent, disclosing any potential conflicts or misconduct, keeping investors informed, and incentivizing positive change. Environmental friendliness encompasses minimal usage of natural resources, a reliance on alternative forms of energy and "clean" technologies, and an acknowledgment that global warming is real. Examples of addressing social issues are creating safer work environments, treating people of color fairly, and having a progressive stance toward females.[38]

While not philanthropy per se, ESG investing is a way to use one's money to benefit society, explaining its sharp rise over the past few years. In fact, most people surveyed in a recent Nielsen survey are willing to sacrifice some financial returns for sustainable offerings. (The jury is still out on whether socially responsible companies perform as well as others from a financial standpoint, but most experts agree that there is not much of a statistical difference.) ESG investments grew 76 percent between 2012 and 2014 in the United States, from $3.74 trillion to $6.57 trillion. There are now more than one hundred "sustainable" mutual funds in the country, offering investors a wider range of stocks and bonds from which to choose. Investors are particularly interested in companies that have reduced carbon footprints, reflecting the growing concern over climate change (i.e., global warming). Companies that use less energy and emit less waste are also at least in theory more efficient, something that should help improve their bottom line.[39]

Best of all, both baby boomers and millennials are keen on supporting socially responsible companies, making ESG investing something that is helping to bridge the generations. "The multigenerational, broad-based appeal of values-based investing, along with an increased focus on sustainability and other social issues within the U.S., makes it easy to understand why demand for these types of investments has skyrocketed in the last 10 years," Scott Stanley of Pharos Wealth Management wrote for LinkedIn in 2016, he and other money managers seeing a bullish future for ESG.[40]

Future Trend 39: ESG

Decision-Making and Leadership Platform

Implications

Opting for an ethical portfolio is on the rise.

- Investors are recognizing that money is a powerful incentive to create positive social change.

More companies are being good citizens in order to attract socially aware investors.

- ESG is on the way to being seen as a necessary cost of doing business.

ESG is a means of adding value to largely undifferentiated financial products and services.

- Mission-driven investing is more compelling than the standard risk:return equation.

Other product and service categories are ripe for the ESG concept.

- Any business is capable of embracing and reflecting social responsibility.

Socially responsible investing is an easy and convenient way for the more affluent to feel good about themselves.

- It is a means of justifying being a "have" when there are so many "have nots."

Good corporate citizenship is a good strategy purely on business terms.

- It supports the long-term view that doing the right things will lead to higher profits.

Opportunities

Make sure your company is aligned with ESG standards in order to appeal to investors.

- Subscribe to the Principles for Responsible Investment (PRI).

Embed ESG thinking into your organization and business model.

- Consumers want to partner with socially engaged companies.

(*continued*)

Future Trend 39 (*continued*)

Flaunt your ESG credentials in corporate communications.

- It is a strong selling point and competitive advantage that operates on a global level.

Appoint an ESG champion in your organization.

- Make this person responsible for guiding the company along a socially sensitive path.

Look to measures of sustainability as the most effective means of establishing ESG qualifications.

- Choose reliance on renewable energies and commitment to environmental soundness.

Use ESG as a multigenerational and multicultural marketing strategy.

- It crosses over the outdated demographic boundaries of age, gender, race, and ethnicity.

Future Trend 40: Localization

For every action there is an equal and opposite reaction, Newton's third law of motion states, but the scientist who discovered gravity might as well have been talking about Future Trends. As globalization blankets the four corners of the earth, the opposing force of localization is pushing back, creating a kind of cultural tug of war playing out in fascinating ways. Food is now often a mash-up of dozens or even hundreds of different cuisines that is ideally prepared with locally sourced ingredients, for example, and politics is typically a fusion of global ideologies and local concerns. Travel too has gone this route; more people are interested in globetrotting but want to go off the beaten track to have "authentic" experiences in native habitats, another example of macro meeting micro.

The desire for locally defined things and experiences is a direct response to the spread of global culture. Greater interconnectedness and sharing of ideas around the world is fueling a yearning for that which is not common to everyone, one could say, much of this of course propelled by the Internet. The sheer ubiquity of the online universe—that it can be accessed by anyone anywhere anytime—is making that which is indigenous or homegrown more valuable and thus more sought after. The resurgence in neighborhood life is another reaction to hyper-globalization, I believe; people need to have a sense of place, accounting for the thriving of many local communities here and abroad. Even pride in hometown sports teams seems to me greater than ever, as fans of a particular city (notably Chicago when the Cubs won the 2016 World Series) find meaning in the fate of their local club just because it happens to play in the area.

For businesspeople plotting out their future, goings-on in retail offer valuable lessons for how to, as the saying goes, think global but act local. "As the world economy continues to merge into a single market, a problem that all companies are forced to think about is how to run a global business that is also localised," wrote Tadashi Yanai of Uniqlo in an internal memo to employees, explaining how the fashion brand had to pursue a dual strategy in order to maintain its relevancy and edge. As it expands around the world to become one of the premier global brands in fashion, Uniqlo is making a concerted effort to also tailor stores to their respective local community. At its flagship store on Oxford Street in London, for example, local culture is featured and celebrated to remind customers that they are in a real, unique place to counterbalance the feeling of disorientation that often comes with globalization. "The idea is to have a space devoted to culture that is unique and relevant and brings something back to the community," explained Uniqlo's creative head, aware that the brand's worldwide presence was not a substitute "to be a good citizen and to be a good neighbour in the neighbourhood."[41]

Other retailers such as Nike and lululemon are also eschewing standardization, commodification, and universality to make local stores somehow special. Consistency is all well and good, execs at these companies understand, but something extra is added to the mix when global businesses partner with local institutions and people. Building relationships with consumers happens on an individual basis, the smartest managers know, suggesting there must be some kind of meaningful connection with each and every person on a local level. Combining the efficiencies of a corporate-wide system with the independence and flexibility of local outposts appears to be a winning formula for global retailers, a prescription that other organizations might follow.[42]

Future Trend 40: Localization

Decision-Making and Leadership Platform

Implications

Localization is a foreseeable byproduct of globalization.

- It is a prime example of the ping-pong effect of trends.

Consumer culture is increasingly localized in the search for what is unique and different.

- It is an ironic backlash to marketers' adeptness at making things look and feel familiar and comfortable.

Much of everyday life is now polarized between local and global culture.

- Middle ground is a lackluster place to be.

Specific expressions of localized omniculturalism are likely to be compelling business propositions.

- It is a best-of-both-worlds combination of macro + micro.

Savvier marketers are aware of the power of packaging localized globalization.

- It is a one-two cultural punch.

Localization is adding much-needed texture and diversity to more generic corporate-wide plans and programs.

- It grounds the universal in the particular.

Opportunities

Once again, think global but act local.

- God is in the details.

Translate global strategies into local tactics.

- Offer market-customized programs and promotions.

(continued)

Future Trend 40 (*continued*)

Partner with locally owned businesses and locally known individuals.

- Work with "Sherpas" who can guide the way through the unique cultural dynamics of a community and can provide instant credibility among natives.

Use social media as a form of grassroots marketing.

- Use it as a grapevine to local news and gossip that is heavily relied upon by more passionate community members.

Bring in experts to attract local enthusiasts.

- Exploit the advantage of having a national or international presence.

Support civic ventures and local events.

- This is a relatively inexpensive way to establish neighborliness.

CHAPTER FIVE

~

Scientific Trends

To riff on one of Yogi Berra's more insightful observations, science ain't what it used to be. I remember science as one of my more painful junior high school experiences, but that is nothing at all like what is now taking place in the field and where it is headed. As a nonscientist, I find it nothing short of remarkable to learn the ways in which some very smart people are changing life as we know it. We are living in a golden age of science that rivals that of the Renaissance, it becomes clear from the ten Future Trends in this chapter, each one an adventurous journey worth exploring. Science is going in all sorts of new and exciting directions, many of them devoted to discovering the secrets and mysteries of life itself. The future of science has much to do with revealing the buildings blocks of the physical world and its occupants, whether it be through exploring the makeup of the universe or determining the genomic and neurological architecture of the human body.

The emerging universe of science is rooted in man's eternal curiosity about the world and what may lay beyond. Now, however, scientists are determined not just to gain a better understanding of the workings of life but to use that knowledge in some productive way. Rather than be in the service of the king or a wealthy patron as in Michelangelo's and da Vinci's day, contemporary geniuses are founding start-ups and hitting up billionaires for venture capital. And while the epicenter of science was in certain pockets of Europe half a millennium or so ago, today's scientists are working anywhere and everywhere. Like other great enterprises of our time, science is steeped in collaborations and partnerships, with people from many backgrounds and disciplines coming together in teams. Still, the same kind of entrepreneurial spirit pervades scientific pursuits, with those in the field fully aware that they are on the frontiers of much of our future.

So what are these eggheads in white lab suits actually doing? Data gathering and analysis remain the nuts and bolts of science, but much activity has something to do with leveraging what was arguably the greatest achievement of our lifetime—the decoding of the human genome. DNA is an endless sandbox biologists and others can play in to build new life forms out of the hereditary material all organisms share. Smallness in all its forms is of great interest, in fact; it is only by parsing the foundation of life that we can really understand what makes the whole thing tick and how that research can potentially be used. As well, the human brain is a source of fascination for many scientists, in part because of its indescribable complexity and the fact that we know relatively little about how it functions. The fate of the planet too is deservingly getting much attention due to climate change and our insatiable appetite for energy, as are potential opportunities related to the health and well-being of our aging population.

Whatever the applications, there is an awareness that game changers reside in the yet-to-be-known, making a significant portion of scientific endeavors somewhat of a high-risk, high-return proposition. Scientists in the twenty-first century are interested in not just pushing the envelope but redesigning and reengineering it to create something better and, perhaps, making a fortune doing it. More than in previous eras, science and technology are often being comingled in a kind of tag-team approach intended to turn pure research into commercial products for the marketplace. As always, there are frightening scenarios attached to the forefront of science, but perhaps no more so than today when the very concepts of life and humanity are up for grabs. Still, businesspeople of all stripes have much to learn from what lies ahead in science, and we all can be inspired by the courage to blaze new, unmarked trails.

Future Trend 41: Exploration

Forty years after William Shatner uttered the iconic words, space really does remain the final frontier. Although the original show was set sometime in the twenty-third century, today's star trekkers have ambitious plans to explore strange new worlds, seek out new life and new civilizations, and to boldly go where no man has gone before. The heady days of the space race may be long over, but a new era in exploration is beckoning with the help of drones, self-replicating robots, holograms, augmented reality (AR), and other technological tools right out of science fiction.[1] While the means may be futuristic, the desire to know more about what may or may not be out there is deeply rooted in the past, specifically JFK's commitment for the nation to go the moon by the end of the 1960s.

Indeed, scenarios not unlike those depicted in the 2015 movie *The Martian* may not be too far away. In 2012, NASA's Curiosity Rover landed on Mars, the beginning of what will likely be a major initiative to explore the red planet via helicopter drone. Learning more about Venus is also in NASA's sights, perhaps by a dirigible-like balloon that is inflated by another spacecraft. The agency has already begun to fund a project to voyage through the liquid hydrocarbon-filled oceans of Titan, Saturn's largest moon, via a "submersible autonomous vehicle" (that would be a submarine to you and me). "This craft will autonomously carry out detailed scientific investigations under the surface of Kraken Mare," said Steven Oleson of the agency, the mission intended to lead to "unprecedented knowledge of an extraterrestrial sea and expanding NASA's existing capabilities in planetary exploration to include in-situ nautical operations."[2] Holy H. G. Wells!

Of course, not just NASA but private companies are keen on space exploration, partly because they believe that it can contribute to real-life applications back here on earth. George Whitesides, CEO at Virgin Galactic (and, I'm not making this up, cochair of the Global Future Council on Space Technologies) is perhaps the biggest cheerleader for the scientific exploration of the final frontier. Satellites are being continually improved due to miniaturization, Whitesides explains, and "disaggregation"—breaking down a large goal into smaller, more achievable ones—is proving to be an effective strategy. More than anything else, however, it is the globalization of space exploration and the interest among entrepreneurs that is making this avenue of science so exciting. "It's an opportunity for us to put the best of humanity forward into the future [by] enabling international cooperation, courage, boldness and entrepreneurship," he said in 2017, sounding a lot like President Kennedy (and Captain Kirk).[3]

So what lies ahead for space exploration over the next decade or two? Whitesides envisions not just the commercialization of space tourism but faster-than-a-speeding-bullet trips around earth and humans walking on the surface of Mars or perhaps on asteroids (rocks too small to be considered planets). And besides raising the bar of adventure travel, he adds, space exploration may add to our knowledge of climatology and be a means to create a global broadband system. "Space science will continue to make great advances," Whitesides predicts, seeing the identification of new planets in other galaxies and the discovery of resources in our own solar system as potential gains.[4] Needless to say, the Holy Grail of all exploration—finding life in another part of the universe—is also on the table, an effort NASA intends to pursue via robots with artificial intelligence combing through space.[5]

Future Trend 41: Exploration

Decision-Making and Leadership Platform

Implications

We are on the cusp of another golden age of space exploration.

- It will be a natural evolution of our perpetual search of parts unknown and pushing of geographic boundaries.

Future space exploration is arguably the most ambitious scientific quest to date.

- It is steeped in the enduring values of discovery and curiosity.

Exploration of the universe is the twenty-first-century version of Manifest Destiny.

- Not just expansion is at work but perhaps colonialism and imperialism.

New synergies are being created between science and technology.

- The study of the physical world is being advanced through the application of new tools and methods.

The hows of space exploration are still wide open and up for grabs.

- They are analogous to the Wild West days of the final frontier.

There are many different players on the exploration scene.

- This is a prime example of the emerging business model of globally public and private collaborations.

Opportunities

Explore potential opportunities within what is one of the most interesting areas of life.

- Space has been a source of fascination for millennia that has attracted some of each era's best and brightest minds.

Consider getting in on the ground floor of space exploration.

- All kinds of partnerships, especially with NASA, are potentially in play.

(continued)

Future Trend 41 (*continued*)

Look to science fiction for cues to actual developments in space exploration.

- Creative interpretations of the future are often more prescient than analytical models.

Develop technologies that will advance space science.

- What kinds of things can make objects go farther and work better?

Utilize the concept of disaggregation.

- This is a good way to make the impossible possible.

Integrate core pillars of space exploration into your organization culture.

- Utilize discovery, imagination, boldness, entrepreneurship, and pushing of the envelope.

Future Trend 42: Genomics

A decade and a half after the completion of the Human Genome Project (to the tune of $3 billion), the field of genomics is exploding as more biopreneurs jump into the fray. Businesspeople are figuring out different ways to capitalize on that historic achievement, especially now that gene sequencing costs just around $1,000 a pop. Evolving technologies and ever-growing mounds of data are other reasons why genomics (that part of molecular biology focused on the structure, function, evolution, and mapping of genomes) is one of the darlings of Wall Street and the venture community.[6] A genome is an organism's compete set of DNA (i.e., the hereditary, cellular material found in humans and just about all other forms of life).

Given that genomics is, in nonscientific speak, the end of the line (meaning the ultimate means of understanding what makes an animal or plant tick), it is clear why it is getting a lot of attention from investors (and government regulators such as the FDA and FTC). The payoffs are potentially huge, with a revolution in medicine predicted as the field unfolds. Opportunities include, but are not limited to, customized health care based on an individual's unique genetic code, greater knowledge of future medical outcomes to which one is predisposed, gene-repairing, and advanced methods of biometric identification.[7] "Genomics research holds the key to meeting many of the global healthcare challenges of the years ahead," notes Enakshi Singh of SAP Health, seeing everything from early detection of cancer to treatment of rare diseases through gene medication as coming soon or already here. The big challenge is to integrate data into clinical practice, making that the focus of many health centers and professionals.[8]

While genomics still may be an arcane field to many, that is quickly changing as the science crosses paths with the marketplace. 23andMe, the start-up that offers genetic testing and analysis, has advertised heavily, bringing genomics literally to life. "You are made of cells," 23andMe explains to non-science majors, the company's name coming from the number of pairs of chromosomes in the human body. Even if one has a good idea of his or her ancestral background, reading the detailed report that arrives in the mail (after spitting in a test tube and sending it to the lab) is nothing short of thrilling. (Turns out I'm .1 percent East Asian, a tiny piece of my DNA but still somewhat of a mystery.) The biotech company is moving fast into the health arena by offering consumers the ability to find out how their genetic profile impacts the risk of acquiring diseases such as Alzheimer's and Parkinson's. Other reports from the company include wellness (deep sleep, lactose intolerance, genetic weight) and carrier status (cystic fibrosis, sickle cell disease, hereditary hearing loss), precisely the kinds of ways in which genomics will be applied in the real world in the future.[9]

Also pointing the way to the emerging field of "medtech" is CRISPR, the advanced genome splicing and editing tool, and the UK-based 100,000 Genomes Project, in which that many genomes from about 70,000 people are being sequenced in order to reinvent the ways that people with cancer and rare diseases are cared for and treated. Even tech titans such as Amazon, Google, IBM, Intel, and Microsoft have gotten into the genome mix by making data analysis available on the cloud. "Access to personalized genomics is likely to revolutionize the way patients view preventive medicine and their access to health," wrote Lavinia Ionita, CEO of Omixy, a company committed to "reinventing the check-up" by "taking the most complete picture of your organism."[10]

Future Trend 42: Genomics

Decision-Making and Leadership Platform

Implications
Genomics represent a central part of the emerging scientific revolution.

- A new kind of medicine is being developed.

(continued)

Future Trend 42 (*continued*)

"Medtech" is drawing funding from various sources like bees to honey.

- A good way to judge the relative strength of any Future Trend: follow the money.

It is hard to bet against the future of medicine and health care.

- Aging boomers are interested in maintaining quality of life as long as possible.

There is proof that genomics can be commercialized successfully.

- The company 23andMe is blazing the trail of a direct-to-consumer model.

Partnerships and alliances between scientific and technological players are the wave of the future.

- Data analysis is the key to research interpretation.

Major hurdles of genomics are privacy issues and government regulation.

- No revolution is ever easy.

Opportunities
Investigate start-up, funding, or investing opportunities related to genomics.

- Potential big returns as the field inevitably expands (and then consolidates).

Use 23andMe as a case study demonstrating that science can be both popular and profitable.

- The key is translating knowledge into relevant and meaningful terms.

Trade on the primary deliverable of "medtech": personalization.

- How can your organization contribute to the fact that we are all unique individuals?

Appropriate the field's secondary deliverable: prevention.

- What can your organization do to help predict consumers' likely futures?

(*continued*)

Future Trend 42 (*continued*)

Focus on one application of genomics research to which most people can relate.

- These include sleep, weight, sensory issues, memory, etc.

Look for possible connections between your industry and genomics.

- How can your product or service add to consumers' sense of well-being?

Future Trend 43: Geoengineering

Climatology as we know it is so, well, twentieth century, isn't it? Even predicting the weather is hardly an exact science, as anyone caught without an umbrella during a thundershower can tell you. Creating the weather is a whole different story, however, and something with which more scientists are toying as climate change becomes a growing concern. Geoengineering—the regulation of the global climate through technological methods—is being seen as perhaps the next great achievement of science, equivalent to the medical advances made during the last century that have saved millions, maybe billions of lives. Not just flooding due to global warming but more extreme weather events, such as typhoons and droughts, are reasons that geoengineering is gaining currency as one of the options on the scientific table.[11]

Needless to say, figuring out how to fix a problem caused by a couple of hundred years of releasing greenhouse gases into the atmosphere is not easy. The depth of the oceans and chemical makeup of the atmosphere are not fully known, for starters, making any potential solutions more guesswork than anything else. Still, a few ideas have been floating around the scientific community to adjust the global thermostat, each with its own downside. Placing a giant solar shield in the sky would indeed create a cooler climate, for example, but might prompt flooding and droughts in some parts of the world. Dumping massive amounts of urea-based nutrients or nitrogen fertilizers into the sea to encourage the growth of phytoplankton would in theory take carbon dioxide out of the air, but at the same time possibly trigger a toxic bloom that could be disastrous for marine life. Land-based solutions too are circulating, but these also carry major potential risks.[12]

Despite the Hollywood disaster movie–like scenarios that can result when fooling with Mother Nature, scientists are moving ahead with projects to determine what can be done to save the planet from the effects of further global warming. Shifting from gas-releasing forms of energy to wind and solar sensibly remains the primary means of climate mitigation, but some scientists believe we should be prepared if a true ecological nightmare appears imminent. In what is the largest geoengineering study to date, a team of Harvard scientists has plans to inject the earth's upper atmosphere with "minimal amounts" of aerosols (initially water and then a limestone compound) over the next few years as a means to learn whether a solar-based solution to climate change is feasible. The project is designed to simulate the ways in which a volcanic eruption cools the air, making this test appear to be a less draconian measure than the wilder proposals being considered.[13]

While the Harvard experiment is a drop in the ocean in terms of the magnitude of the problem, so to speak, it is encouraging that the scientific community is doing more than trying to convince lingering naysayers that global warming is real. Most important, perhaps, the once fringe field of geoengineering is moving from theory to practice, something that is attracting the interests of businesspeople. The Bill & Melinda Gates Foundation is one of the principal funders of the Harvard project, for example, and the aerospace industry is curious about its commercial possibilities.[14] As experts in the field ponder such questions as who should be in charge of the earth's climate system and which method should be used if/when we reach the emergency stage, geoengineering continues to become part of the mainstream global scientific community, with many potential opportunities to be had as it evolves over the course of many decades to come.

Future Trend 43: Geoengineering

Decision-Making and Leadership Platform

Implications
The stakes of geoengineering cannot be any higher.

- Saving the planet is a worthy endeavor by any measure.

Geoengineering is following the path of other branches of science.

- First study, then predict, and, finally, alter.

Like Genomics (Future Trend 42), geoengineering is in its early days.

- It is analogous to vaccinations or atomic energy a century or so ago.

(*continued*)

Future Trend 43 (*continued*)

Any and all efforts in geoengineering are literally global in scope.

- Everyone is affected by climate change and rising water levels.

Big money is also potentially at stake.

- Geoengineering is at the intersection of many different parties with a vested interest in stopping global warming.

Some of our best and brightest (and wealthiest) are attracted to the field because of its enormous risks and rewards.

- These are good people and institutions to be around.

Opportunities

Join the ultimate quest to save the world from possible extinction.

- There is no greater mission.

Go to the next level in your own industry by reengineering present conditions.

- Choose a more advanced pursuit than study or even prediction.

Be inspired by the pure audacity and ambitiousness of geoengineering.

- A select group of scientists are literally reaching for the stars.

Do your part to combat global warming.

- Contribute to climate mitigation through the use of alternative energies and other green strategies.

Lobby for all nations and corporations to look for ways to cut or eliminate greenhouse gases.

- Make geoengineering unnecessary.

Put your own Plan B into effect.

- Look for contingencies should the worst-case scenario hit your organization.

Future Trend 44: Longevity

"Longevity turns out to be one of the biggest challenges of the 21st century," writes focusingfuture.com, as scientists try to figure out ways to extend the life of the human body. A number of factors—principally the rise of modern medicine—have pushed the average life span upward for the past couple of centuries, but some are convinced that it can still be increased by decades or more. Researchers at the Albert Einstein College of Medicine believe that as currently configured the human body can last a maximum of 125 years but, of course, none of us make it that far. So how can another half-century or so be tacked on to the average life span? longevity experts wonder, sensibly thinking that finding new cures to infectious and chronic diseases represent the biggest potential gains.[15]

Continuing along this tried-and-true path rooted in the amazing scientific achievements of the twentieth century does not preclude taking another path that may lead to equally remarkable discoveries, however. Rather than crawl up to 125 years or more, exponential leaps in longevity are feasible, some believe, with emerging fields such as bionic and synthetic biology potentially offering decades-long hops. And as Future Trend 42 showed, modifying DNA is being made possible through genomics, something that can perhaps rewrite the very rules of the game. "Adjustment of the source code of life itself allows humanity to extend life through a variety of means," focusingfuture.com continues, with new cell generation and bioprinting potential methods to grow replacement bodily organs as the old ones break down. Swapping out body parts with mechanical ones is another way to possibly increase longevity dramatically, as Future Trend 50 shows, this too buoying researchers' hopes that a breakthrough may be near.[16]

For a better understanding of the future of longevity, there's no better place to look than the Buck Institute in the Bay Area. The institute is entirely devoted to learning ways to not just add years to the back end of life but improve health as well, that is, a dual effort focused on both quantity (life span) and quality (health span). Researchers at the University of Michigan, the University of Texas, and the University of California at San Francisco are also investigating methods to put the brakes on the aging process, as is the Mayo Clinic. Google too has entered the fray with its billions of cash by forming the California Life Company (aka Calico) which is situated in the longevity space but reveals little about its work, and Craig Venter, the biotech entrepreneur, has also entered the "de-aging" scene.[17]

Given that scientists still don't even know exactly why we age (an organism bent on destroying itself goes against the survivalist principles of biology), the dream of all of us becoming centenarians remains an elusive one. There is a long and unimpressive history attached to the search for a fountain of youth, of course, hard evidence that encourages a healthy dose of skepticism toward the efforts of modern Ponce de Leons. As well, extending the life of a yeast, worm, or mouse is a lot different from that of a human being, yet more reason to view longevity research as a scientific bon-bon among those with excessive amounts of money in their pockets. But like other grand ventures in the realm of science, attempting to make human life longer and better can be seen as a noble pursuit very much worth exploring, even if it does not lead to the utopian aspirations of those in the field. Count on man's centuries-long battle against aging to escalate in the future as new kinds of science promise to answer some of the riddles of life itself.

Future Trend 44: Longevity

Decision-Making and Leadership Platform

Implications

Attempts to increase longevity are a running theme in the human experience.

- It is a staple of both mythology and science.

Futile attempts to date cast reasonable doubt on future efforts.

- Some of the mysteries of life may simply be beyond human comprehension.

Researchers working in the longevity space are undeterred by the less-than-impressive accomplishments of their predecessors.

- A new generation of scientists is working with new tools and techniques.

Longevity is connected directly to genomics and other revolutionary branches of biology.

- There is still much to be learned from the decoding of the human genome.

Learnings related to health span are more important and valuable than those of life span.

- Quality of life > quantity of life.

(continued)

Future Trend 44 (*continued*)

All kinds of ethical and moral issues are embedded in efforts to extend human life dramatically.

- Do we really want to live 125 years?

Opportunities
Take on one of the biggest challenges of the twenty-first century.

- The leading edge of science is ideally aligned with man's eternal quest to live as long as possible.

Consider investing in longevity research.

- Big, smart money is doing the same.

Rub elbows with some of the elite scientists of the day.

- What can your organization bring to the longevity party?

Plan for the long-term possibility of many longer-living human beings.

- What kind of wants and needs can your company fill for an older but healthier population?

Create your own "de-aging" product or service.

- How can you increase consumers' health spans?

Steer clear of the "anti-aging" category promising to slow or reverse the aging process.

- Nothing besides radical calorie restriction has yet to prove effective.

Future Trend 45: Nanoscience

Nanoscience—the study of objects, structures, and materials at the nano, or one-billionth level—has been around now for more than two decades, but it is only recently that research in the field is paying off. Nanoscience, and its more applied cousin nanotechnology, is transforming many different arenas of society including food safety, energy, transportation, medicine, and homeland security. Designing the makeup of materials at the super-micro level is an ideal means to endow products with certain properties; this makes nanoscience such a promising field for the future. Attributes such as strength, lightness, and durability are much desired in the marketplace, the reason that manufacturing on a nanoscale has taken off in clothing, electronics, vehicles, household and personal care products, and many others. The Internet of Things—the exchange of data by objects—is also heavily reliant on nanoscience, more reason to believe that the field will expand in the future as machines increasingly communicate with each other.[18]

A team of researchers at UCLA has a keen sense of how nanoscience will likely evolve over the next decade and how learnings in the field will translate into new technologies. In medicine, nanoparticles may be capable of pinpointing specific areas of the body with an infectious disease, where they would release powerful drugs to combat bacteria and viruses. (In this scenario it's difficult not to be reminded of how a submarine carrying a crew is shrunk to microscopic size and injected into the body of an injured scientist to save his life in the 1966 film *Fantastic Voyage*.) Better ways to treat Alzheimer's and Parkinson's diseases and arthritis could result from further strides in nanoscience, they believe, as can new methods to fight cancer through the ability of nanoscale particles to work with the body to destroy tumor cells.[19]

The $500 billion microelectronics business is equally excited about the possibilities nanoscience offers in terms of data processing and storage, and the energy industry too sees big gains to be made through greater sustainability and efficiencies. Both water and air are currently being purified via nano-based technologies, but there is still much room for growth in this area on a global scale. In food manufacturing, nanosensors can be woven into the design of products to detect contamination or spoilage so people don't get sick after eating them. Perhaps the greatest strength of nanoscience is its breadth of applications and cross-disciplinary approach. As with many Future Trends, nanoscience is a collaborative effort, with people from a wide spectrum of academic backgrounds working together to move the field ahead. "The field is poised to make contributions far beyond the nanoscale worlds that we have explored so far," says Paul Weiss, a member of UCLA's team, thinking, "this is the age of discovery for nanoscience and nanotechnology."[20]

Scientists are indeed thinking big about the potential uses of nano. Folks at the three Kavli nanoscience institutes envision things such as teleportation and invisibility cloaks as one day possibly becoming real through nanodesign. Less like *Star Trek* but similarly impressive are the advances to be made in artificial photosynthesis, quantum computing, and superfast genome analysis, they believe. "I'm hoping that people will look back on this moment as a very special one, because this was when nanoscience began to change the way we look at the world," observed Paul Alivisatos of Kavli, describing the field as "like a movement, a new way of thinking and bringing things together."[21]

Future Trend 45: Nanoscience
Decision-Making and Leadership Platform

Implications
"Smallness" is allowing new possibilities within a plethora of industries.

- The future is "The Next Small Thing" versus "The Next Big Thing."

It is typical to take a generation to translate new scientific findings into applied technologies.

- The marketplace will soon be flooded with nano-designed products and techniques.

Virtually anything can benefit from being made stronger, lighter, and more durable.

- A revolution in manufacturing is taking place.

The capabilities of nanoscience are beyond the comprehension of not just laypeople but experts in the field.

- Much of the field still resides in the uncharted territories of science.

Nanoscience is benefiting from a cross-cultural and interdisciplinary approach.

- These are different but complementary ways of thinking.

The field of nanoscience is capable of making real, measurable contributions to society.

- There is the usual caveat involving dangers and risks of anything truly innovative.

Opportunities
Think small.

- The relative capabilities of seemingly everything reside in design at super-micro level.

Invest in nanoscience as it becomes increasingly commercialized.

- Superior specifications, features, and benefits = competitive advantages.

(continued)

Future Trend 45 (*continued*)

Apply the model of neuroscience to your own industry.

- Work from the bottom up versus top down for greater sustainability and efficiencies.

Approach your organizational goal setting in a nanoscientific manner.

- Target micro versus macro areas of opportunity.

Take a cross-cultural, interdisciplinary approach in your business.

- Making connections across boundaries is a primary means to breakthrough innovation and success.

Look to your business as a kind of movement demanding a new way of thinking.

- A higher calling can become a self-fulfilling prophecy.

Future Trend 46: Neuroscience

While space may be the final frontier, neuroscience represents the exploration of the human brain, an equally exciting endeavor filled with many unknowns. Neuroscience is the study of the structure and function of not just the brain but the nervous system, the most complex network in the body. The field as we know it can be said to have been around in one form or another for about a half-century now, when automation advanced B. F. Skinner's famous experiments of the 1940s investigating how and why organisms behave the way they do.[22] Neuroscience today demands a solid grasp of molecular biochemistry and cognitive psychology as well as excellent computing chops, making it one of the more challenging fields on which to embark.[23]

Understanding the workings of the human mind is now more relevant than ever, however, due in part to the rising epidemic of Alzheimer's disease and physicians' commitment to treat other brain disorders such as epilepsy and autism more effectively. Urgency notwithstanding, making major progress in neuroscience is a bit like pushing the proverbial snowball uphill, the simple reason being the not-at-all-simple nature of the brain. Even the normal flow through the nervous system resembles the human traffic pattern of Grand Central Station at rush hour, with streams of information going in all directions all at once. (There are about 86 billion neurons in the human brain.) Mapping out the cognitive geography of the brain, documenting its continuous activity as it tells the rest of the body what to do, and determining the types of cells in our noggins are all goals neuroscientists have their sights on. As well, artificial intelligence is gradually bumping into neuroscience as the lines between man and machine get blurrier.[24]

Like other hugely ambitious undertakings, neuroscience research is benefiting from some very generous gifts from some very rich benefactors. (Paul Allen, the cofounder of Microsoft, funds the Allen Institute for Brain Science to the tune of $500 million.)[25] Big money is typically needed to pay for "big data," that form of statistics in which tremendously large sets of information are analyzed by computer algorithms. Companies in many industries have used big data for some time now to turn patterns and correlations into profits, but more recently neuroscientists are relying on it to gain, as Francis Collins of the National Institutes of Health put it, a "dynamic understanding of brain function." As in other scientific fields, gathering large amounts of data is the relatively easy part; analyzing it is a different story entirely, however, making that a primary initiative in the future of neuroscience.[26]

Also, as in other arenas where the rules have yet to be written, major ethical issues surround potential achievements in neuroscience. Would it be acceptable to boost an individual's cognitive powers, say, should that be possible one day? How about modifying a person's memories or, perhaps, reading someone's mind should neuroscience research lead to that ability? Neuroethicists—yes, there is such a job title—are pondering such questions as the field enters unfamiliar terrain.[27] Despite such ethical quandaries, there is little doubt that neuroscience will play a much bigger role in our future. Exploring the architecture of the brain and the biology that makes it run is a privilege to which many people will be drawn. "The more scientists learn about the brain, the more questions arise and the more challenging the quest to understand human thinking becomes," wrote Bahar Gholipour for livescience.com, a very good way to describe the exhilarating possibilities of neuroscience.[28]

Future Trend 46: Neuroscience

Decision-Making and Leadership Platform

Implications
The human brain is still largely a mystery.

- There is still much to be learned about how we think and why we act.

Neuroscience is as complex and challenging a field as any.

- Studying the brain is not for the faint of heart.

(continued)

Future Trend 46 (*continued*)

There is a new urgency attached to neuroscience.

- Alzheimer's disease is already an epidemic and will rise dramatically over the next decades as baby boomers age.

Neuroscience is gradually spinning off neurotechnology.

- Research will be applied to the development of smart machines powered by artificial intelligence.

Wealthy technology philanthropists are backing neuroscience research.

- This is a natural fit for billionaires who made their fortunes in the information business.

Translating data into useful findings is the next big step in neuroscience.

- How can and should research be used to benefit individuals and society?

Opportunities
Apply learnings from neuroscience research to your business.

- Thinking and acting—the basis of decision making and leadership— is the foundation of any organization.

Integrate psychological theory with empirical science for a better understanding of the workings of the human mind.

- Sigmund Freud was a neurologist before founding psychoanalysis.

Seek out opportunities revolving around the reality of millions more aging minds.

- What products and services can help boomers' cognitive abilities?

Make brain disorders your organization's philanthropic cause.

- A war on Alzheimer's disease will soon be waged.

Sponsor a professorial chair in neuroscience at an institution of your choice.

- This is a good way to advance the field and network with some heavy hitters.

Explore relevant possibilities of artificial intelligence.

- Smart machines are coming whether we want them or not.

Future Trend 47: Renewables

What has taken place in the global energy industry in just the past decade is nothing short of remarkable. Future historians will view the Paris Agreement of 2016 as a landmark event not just as related to energy but in world affairs, I believe, as nations came together to acknowledge the environmental plight of the planet. Today, renewable energy—power from a source that is not depleted when used, such as wind or solar—represents 86 percent of all new power systems in the European Union, according to the 2017 Renewables Global Futures Report. China, of all places, is taking a leadership role in the push toward renewable energy, quite surprising given its less-than-laudable environmental track record. As well, more than half of the money going into renewables is being directed to emerging markets in developing nations, this too something that would have been difficult to predict not that long ago.[29]

President Trump's decision for the United States to opt out of that agreement notwithstanding, "there is consensus that we have to radically re-consider how we produce and consume energy," the report issued by the Renewable Energy Policy Network for the 21st Century (REN21) stated, the ultimate goal being to prevent additional global warming. To achieve that, the energy industry must move toward total decarbonization, REN21 (a global network of renewable energy policymakers) asserts, a major challenge given the number of players involved and their disparate interests. Still, realizing a 100 percent renewable energy by the mid-twenty-first century is entirely possible, the organization believes, with partnerships between the public and private sectors to make this happen.[30]

Trump's decision to back out of the Paris Agreement was surprising not just because Nicaragua and Syria were the only countries to not sign the accord but because it is likely that the United States can get close to REN21's goal of total decarbonization by 2050. A recent study by the National Renewable Energy Laboratory or NREL (part of the Department of Energy) reported that renewables can provide 80 percent of our electricity by mid-century, with about 50 percent to come from solar and wind power and the remainder from other technologies such as hydropower, geothermal, and biopower. Importantly, renewables would be able to meet electricity demand coast-to-coast and 24/7, assuming of course that such a scenario were supported by both the energy industry and the powers that be. "Ultimately, the U.S. needs a long-term clean energy policy that creates a long-term market for renewable energy, encourages and supports the integration of renewable energy, puts a price on carbon emissions, and increases funding for research and development," the NREL states, steps that other countries are already taking.[31]

One might look to New York State to see the future of energy in this country and elsewhere. New York is already constructing the next generation's energy grid by investing $5 billion in clean forms of power, an initiative that state officials believe will result not just in less carbon in the air but in more jobs. California, Hawaii, and Massachusetts are also charging toward renewables, but New York is changing the fundamentals of the energy business that has long incentivized utility companies for peddling as much electricity as possible. By financially rewarding utilities in various ways for moving to a cleaner grid, the state is becoming a magnet for energy start-ups and, in the process, creating all kinds of new employment opportunities. New York is proving that renewables can be a win-win scenario, a view that is destined to become the norm.[32]

Future Trend 47: Renewables

Decision-Making and Leadership Platform

Implications
Renewable energy is the wave of both the future and the present.

- States and nations with foresight are gradually converting grids.

There is a virtual consensus among countries that carbon-based energies are a relic of the past.

- The global scientific community agrees that the temperature of earth has risen.

Smart money is being put on renewable energy.

- The public and the private sector each view the conversion process as an opportunity versus a cost.

Financial incentives are required for utilities to alter the status quo.

- Pressure for profits encourages short-term thinking.

The wide variety of renewables is a big plus.

- Different areas demand different kinds of energy sources.

Policy has yet to catch up to the science and technology of renewable energy in the United States.

- Utility lobbyists and governmental bureaucracy are resistant to change.

(continued)

Future Trend 47 (*continued*)

Opportunities
Be a champion for renewable energy.

- It is highly unlikely that hundreds of thousands of scientists are wrong about the dangers of climate change.

Look to agreement about carbon emissions as an opportunity to display global citizenship.

- Power resides in being part of the coming together of nations.

Lobby local, state, and federal officials to make energy policies friendly to renewables.

- Change accelerates when both bottom-up and top-down forces are at work.

Go to school on New York State's approach to seeding a culture of innovation.

- Environmentalism is a very worthy cause but money talks.

Convert your organization's energy system to one relying on renewables.

- Be recognized as one of the greenest companies in your industry and state.

Provide incentives for your employees and the public to invest in renewables.

- Offer discounts or premiums (or simple recognition) for going partly solar.

Future Trend 48: Sustainability

"Environmental change drives social transformations," writes the United Nations Educational, Scientific and Cultural Organization (UNESCO), correctly arguing that negative forces such as global warming, diminishing biodiversity, lack of fresh water, poor management of waste, soil degradation, and air pollution have deep impact on real people's lives. Likewise, "social transformations drive environmental change," UNESCO continues, with what and how people consume having a direct effect on quality of life. For each of these reasons, sustainability science—the study of the relationship among physical, biological, and social systems in order to promote positive change—is gaining considerable traction.[33] While a relatively new field, sustainability science will become an increasingly important one as policy makers struggle with the planet's many environmental and social challenges. The field is an interdisciplinary fusion of the humanities and social sciences, with over one hundred colleges and universities in the United States offering programs for students interested in careers related to sustainability.[34]

Making an academic discipline out of the fuzzy concept of sustainability is itself quite an achievement. The goal of sustainability science is indeed a bold one: to make scientific research and education more directly address and find potential solutions to the complex problems of the world. Historically, scientists have tended to stay within the parameters of their own discipline and area of specialization and, more often than not, preferred to stay within the comfortable confines of academia versus trying to confront the seemingly overwhelming problems of the real world. That is fast changing with sustainability science, as practitioners confront not just environmental issues but those related to poverty and conflict as well.[35]

The idea to create a new form of science in order to address the world's most complex problems is indeed a daring one. But universities and grant-making agencies are increasingly demanding that scientists make their work relevant and useful in an applied sense; research should not be just for research's sake, in other words, but contribute to society in some way. Much funding comes from taxpayers' pockets, after all, making such a requirement not as wacky as it may seem. Sustainability science goes after the big fish in the pond, however, in part by researchers' commitment to meet face to face with the people who are most affected by serious problems in their everyday lives. "Sustainability science programs must be interdisciplinary in order to increase the scope of its research capabilities, be applicable to real-world problems while contributing to discovery-based science, and be integrated into society," explains Benjamin P. Warner of the University of Massachusetts–Amherst, thinking the field was nothing less than "academia's saving grace."[36]

The Sustainability Science Program at Harvard's Kennedy School of Government serves as a prime model for what the field is about and why it represents a true pivot point in the history of science. The grand mission of that program is to "foster shared prosperity and reduced poverty while protecting the environment" by "advancing scientific understanding of human-environment systems, improving connections between research and policy communities, and building capacity for linking knowledge with action to promote sustainability." Dense language and with good reason, as the field draws people from many different backgrounds and supports many kinds of initiatives residing at the intersection of the environment and development. Expect this kind of problem-driven research to sweep through science and academia in the future.[37]

Future Trend 48: Sustainability

Decision-Making and Leadership Platform

Implications
Sustainability is a key concept in science and beyond.

- The relationship between people and the planet is a growing concern.

The field of sustainability is about not just environmental issues but their economic consequences.

- It illustrates the interconnected nature of the more complex problems of the world.

The science of sustainability is understandably gaining recognition in academia, government, and business.

- It is at the crossroads of many disciplines and global in scope.

Practicality has historically been a revolutionary idea in science and academia overall.

- The urgency of sustainability is now shaking up the ivory tower.

Practitioners are not afraid to get into the proverbial trenches.

- Their focus is on real problems of real people.

Purpose- and problem-driven initiatives will receive the greatest support from funding sources.

- Its relevancy is more important than ever.

Opportunities
Plant the concept of sustainability in your organization's ecosystem.

- Integrate environmental responsibility, economic equity, and peacefulness in your company's charter.

(continued)

Future Trend 48 (*continued*)

Strive toward positive social transformation by instilling sustainability into your objectives and strategies.

- Help change the world for the better while achieving corporate goals.

Draw inspiration from sustainability scientists' bending (or breaking) of the rules.

- Confront the most complex problems of your own industry.

Embrace the radical concept of practical, purpose-driven problem solving.

- Make measurable results a priority.

Name a CSO in your organization.

- CSO = Chief Sustainability Officer.

Reach out to people outside your industry and business who share similar goals.

- Synergies can be gained from complementary thinking.

Future Trend 49: Synthetics

Synthetic biology is "the field of the future," according to Jay Keasling of UC Berkeley, explaining why that particular science will be better known and appreciated in the years to come. For the last decade or two, synthetic biology has been used to produce new organisms by trading on the genetic revolution allowing the synthesis and sequencing of DNA. Like most scientific Future Trends, the field of synthetics takes a multidisciplinary approach with not just biologists but software developers, engineers, and others joining forces to turn different genetic components into something functional. The emergence of synthetic biology is one reason scientists are pronouncing that we are on the cusp of a "bioeconomy" (i.e., economy driven by findings in the biosciences).[38]

The range of applications of the new science is truly remarkable. In the medical arena, for example, synthetic biology is being used to create microbes that can eradicate tumors before themselves committing suicide, much like the mission of a kamikaze pilot. The science has environmental applications as well, with organisms capable of eating up toxic, decomposition-resistant chemicals in soil or water. Significant advances in producing food will also likely be made from synthetic biology as researchers figure out a way to alter the chemistry of plants to make using fertilizer no longer necessary to grow crops. And by turning bacteria like *E. coli* into a microbial sweatshop, massive amounts of biofuels can be created on the cheap, another reason that more members of the scientific community are gravitating toward synthetics. "We envision that eventually we will be able to build just about anything from biology," Keasling notes, not too surprising really given the field's basis in the building blocks of life itself.[39]

Marketers are already capitalizing on scientists' ability to reengineer bacteria, yeast, and other cells to create products that are somehow superior to what can be made in a typical factory or by nature itself. Gingko Bioworks in Boston, for example, is reprogramming yeast to create different varietals of rose oil for the fragrance industry, resulting in new, unique scents never sniffed before.[40] Spiber Inc., a Japanese biomaterials company, meanwhile, has redesigned bacteria to produce a stronger, lighter version of spider silk for use in cold-weather clothing. And at the Swiss Federal Institute of Technology, scientists are "wiring" cells to create circuits with biomedical sensors. These "living pills" can not only identify areas of disease in the blood but also release healing substances, preventing further damage. "Biology has given us this big, crazy library of stuff to choose from," observed Christopher Voigt, a synthetic biologist at MIT, with more than 190 million DNA sequences from 100,000 organisms from which to choose.[41]

Needless to say, creating new life forms has scientists both excited and concerned about where synthetic biology might go. In her book *Synthetic: How Life is Made*, Sophia Roosth, a historian of science at Harvard, posits that the very definition of what constitutes an organism or defines a species is up for grabs. Synthetic biologists are in effect taking control of the process of evolution, with the reengineering of life a radical (and scary) proposition at any level. But Roosth reminds us that in the early DNA research of the 1970s, some were worried that scientists were "playing God" by intervening in the stuff of life. Likewise, synthetic biology will soon be seen as "a commonsense approach to bioengineering," she predicts, and, in the process, "become both less surprising and more thinly spread across the life sciences."[42]

Future Trend 49: Synthetics

Decision-Making and Leadership Platform

Implications

Synthetic biology is reinventing the process of evolution.

- It is altering the foundation of life as we know it.

The field of synthetics is one of a number of new sciences growing out of the sequencing of the human genome.

- Synthesizing life is a predictable extension of decades of genetic research.

The promise of synthetics is attracting more scientists from traditional molecular biology and other fields.

- The potential applications are seemingly boundless.

The marketplace is increasingly receptive to synthetics.

- A bioscience-based "bioeconomy" is emerging.

Many start-ups are intent on "improving" nature via genetic engineering.

- All kinds of possibilities are feasible when starting at the cellular level.

There are understandable concerns about fooling with Mother Nature.

- There is no real precedent in synthesizing biology.

Opportunities

Leverage the concept of synthetics in your business.

- Create synthetic, custom-engineered products that are superior in some way to the real thing.

Find a niche in the blossoming bioeconomy.

- True innovation and genuine breakthroughs are increasingly possible through bioscience.

Seek out new opportunities grounded in the genetics revolution.

- What else can be done through the sequencing of DNA?

(continued)

Future Trend 49 (*continued*)

Consider putting venture money into bioscience or biotech.

- Synthetics is clearly a "field of the future."

Form teams of people from different disciplines and backgrounds.

- Great ideas reside in connections otherwise unseen.

Challenge conventional ways of doing things in your own industry.

- If creating new life forms is possible, anything is.

Future Trend 50: Transhumanism

"Are you ready for the future of transhumanism?" asks *Huffington Post* blogger Zoltan Istvan, then telling readers that they had better be. The ability to go beyond the biology of our bodies is already here, of course, although current transhumanism is small potatoes to what is coming around the bend. Night-vision-equipped contact lenses, artificial limbs capable of picking up a refrigerator, and brain implants that can tell others what you are thinking are all on the near horizon as nonhuman elements are combined with our bodies. Brain activity can be detected by electroencephalography (EEG) sensors and then relayed via NeuroSky's MindWave, for example, and there have even been successful demonstrations of telepathy or mind-to-mind communication.[43]

It is, however, within the field of medicine that transhumanism may play the biggest role. Installing a microchip into one's brain can help rebuild a person's memory, preliminary research shows, something that could prove to be a primary weapon in the burgeoning war being declared on Alzheimer's disease. "A thriving pro-cyborg medical industry is setting the stage for trillion-dollar markets that will remake the human experience," Istvan continues, with prosthetics and robotic implants part of the emerging arena of science-based "radical tech."[44] As in synthetic science, transhumanism is making the definition of a human being not so clear as the boundaries of our physical selves are expanded. While transhumanism has actually been around in some form for a long time (drugs, vitamins, hearing aids, heart pacemakers, and hip and knee replacements can be seen as the nonhumanization of humans), a new scientific era promising to augment or expand our cognitive and sensory abilities awaits.[45]

Alongside science-based radical tech, smart drugs or nootropics represent the future of transhumanism. Ever since the first person chewed on a coffee bean and found himself or herself talking much faster, chemistry in one form or another has been used to alter or enhance the performance of our minds and bodies. We may still drink espresso to get going in the morning, but a new generation of drugs and supplements, both natural and synthetically derived, could one day be as ubiquitous as Starbucks. Nootropics—substances that can boost cognitive abilities—are already gaining popularity as a means to help our brains process information better and/or faster. Enthusiasts of nootropics (many of them in tech-obsessed Silicon Valley) consume a customized cocktail of such substances in order to optimize their powers of cognition, something many more of us may soon be doing. Common nootropics include fish oil, creatine, and L-theanine (an amino acid often found in green tea), while the more exotic belong to a group of drugs called "racetams."[46]

Will nootropics turn us all into the kind of genius seen in the 2011 film *Limitless* after the Bradley Cooper character takes his magic pill? Hardly. Nootropics work cumulatively rather than instantly, proponents make clear, and may offer a bump of perhaps 10 percent in cognition, specifically that related to attention, alertness, and the ability to switch gears. But being continually 10 percent more intelligent or productive can mean the difference between success or failure, however defined, a powerful incentive for many of us to sign up. The neuroscience behind nootropics is so far not clear, but advances in that field will no doubt lead to a better understanding of if and how smart drugs actually work.[47] Expect nootropics to evolve into a legitimate field of its own as Big Pharma looks for new opportunities to make big money.

Future Trend 50: Transhumanism

Decision-Making and Leadership Platform

Implications

Humans are destined to go further beyond their natural biology.

- There is a long history of altering our bodies both internally and externally through chemistry and devices.

Radical-tech is finding real applications in the marketplace.

- Science is being used to develop body-enhancing or even Superman-like technologies.

(*continued*)

Future Trend 50 (*continued*)

Much of transhumanism is understandably focused on the brain.

- There is significant interest in ways to improve one's cognitive abilities.

Brain implants are offering great possibilities in medicine.

- A killer app is needed for the Alzheimer's epidemic.

Smart drugs are gradually creeping into everyday life.

- More people are interested in gaining some kind of cognitive edge.

Transhumanism is blurring the lines between man and machine.

- Mechanically augmented bodies will one day seem entirely normal.

Opportunities

The plan for more advanced forms of transhumanism will become a reality.

- It is part of the inevitable march of science and technology.

Offer consumers ways to augment their body's natural abilities.

- Many if not most people are interested in maximizing their cognitive and physical powers.

Look to Starbucks as an early form of commercialized transhumanism.

- Caffeine is regarded as a safe, socially acceptable brain booster when packaged into a delicious beverage.

Explore alternative paths for individuals to be more than they can ordinarily be.

- Non-chemistry-based methods will go far beyond the bodies into which we were born.

Target a specific area of potential physical improvement.

- Focus on enhanced sensory ability, stronger immune system, etc.

Acknowledge the widening parameters of what is and isn't considered real.

- Perception is becoming the new reality in many arenas of life.

CHAPTER SIX

~

Technological Trends

So I go to the drive-through of my local McDonald's the other day and I'm greeted not by a garbled human voice but an automated, Siri-like one. There are actual human employees inside the restaurant but not for long, I'm thinking; if there's one thing that robots excel at, it's completing repetitive tasks such as filling orders without getting tired (or asking for a raise, health insurance, or help with college tuition). A fair percentage of the time what I get in my bag is not what I ordered, more reason that a machine will likely replace people in any kind of job demanding speed, efficiency, and accuracy.

If Mickey D's—the most popular restaurant in the world—becomes robotized, the writing is on the wall in terms of the presence of technology in our lives. Over the course of the past couple of centuries or so, technology of one kind or another has ensconced itself in virtually every aspect of our everyday existence, so much so that it has become the dominant feature in many people's lives. (I'd venture that a fair share of folks spends more time with their various electronic devices than with other human beings.) And unlike the Future Trends in the other chapters of this book, those based in technology (the application of scientific knowledge for practical purposes, especially in industry) are advancing exponentially, meaning they progress in a continually steeper versus consistently linear way. There is no question that technology is deeply altering the ways in which we do things, with even greater reshaping of things to come. Robots and other forms of automation are indeed coming to our home, workplace, and the marketplace, posing major implications for the role of humans in the future. Machines are increasingly being incorporated into our biology, transforming the nature of humanity itself, and trends such as predictives, quantum, and virtuality point to a tomorrow that will be much different from today.

As well, as technology gets smaller and smarter, machines are more frequently interfacing with each other, creating a web of connectivity that very well may become the framework for life as we know it. Indeed, if there is one common element residing in this relentless pursuit of better and better technology, it is intelligence. We've gotten very good at getting machines to do things but haven't quite figured out how to make them think, at least on their own. This is the ultimate objective of technology (and perhaps humankind), and one that many of the smartest people alive are determined to achieve. The prospect of machines that can think (and maybe feel) like or better than humans smacks of the kind of dystopian nightmares of science fiction, but history has shown that technology is rarely if ever completely bad (or good). As usual, the benefits that machines of the future will provide will be countered by the financial, social, and emotional costs involved by our tendency to rely on them for too much.

Meanwhile, it's revenge of the quants, as technologists take on some of the biggest challenges of our time and try to find solutions for some of our biggest problems. As in science, data is the lifeblood of technology, and, as more and more is corralled, figuring out what it means and what to do next is a big part of the emerging technological scene. Not just waiting for the future to happen but to proactively manage it by anticipating likely scenarios based on data is another major initiative within the realm of technology. Creating alternative realities will be increasingly relied upon to foresee and plan for possible events or situations, just one way in which immersive technologies will represent a big part of our collective future. Overall, these are heady days for technology, this chapter makes clear, as we witness what I believe to be our most determined effort to invent new and better tools in order to make life better.

Future Trend 51: Automation

Yes, the bots are indeed coming. Much has been made of our robotic future, and there can be no doubt that the years in front of us will be greatly automated. Automation will affect society in all kinds of ways, but perhaps no more so than in the workplace. "How long will it be before you lose your job to a robot?" Elizabeth Kolbert asked recently in the New Yorker; the common answer provided by experts in the field is "soon." A team at Oxford University reported in 2013 that almost half of the jobs in America are "potentially automatable" in possibly "a decade or two," making the prospect of a largely people-less workplace in the not-so-distant future not that farfetched.[1]

The fear that machines will make humans superfluous goes back centuries, and with good reason. Labor-intensive industries such as textiles and agriculture became heavily automated during the Industrial Revolution, but many jobs in those occupations shifted to factories and offices. With the advent of robots, however, there may not be such a parallel transfer of employment; it appears they will be quite capable of managing themselves.[2] The difference this time around, historians of technology point out, is that the Digital Revolution threatens to make not just many blue-collar jobs obsolete but a good number of white-collar ones as well. "Automation may also affect middle-income jobs, such as clerks, chefs, office workers, security guards, junior lawyers, inspectors," noted Richard Gray of BBC Future Now in 2017, considering the robotization of the human workforce one of the "grand challenges facing humanity." Automation is already altering the employment landscape of health care, the legal industry, Wall Street, and many other arenas, making such concerns entirely justifiable.[3]

Given such a depressing scenario, it's not surprising that human resource people and others have offered ways to "future-proof" one's job. The traditional model of employment, in which one prepared for a career and then pursued it by doing essentially the same thing for decades, will no longer be viable in a workplace profoundly defined by automation and artificial intelligence. (The freelance or gig economy will also wreak havoc with that model, as Future Trend 17 showed.) Instead, continually acquiring new skills will become the norm, suggesting that learning, as opposed to actually working, will take up a large percentage of our professional lives. And according to McKinsey and Company, very few of us will be completely replaced by robots; even they will not be capable of doing all the things that humans do in a given workday. Rather, we are likely to work alongside robots in a kind of job-sharing capacity in the future, they believe, a much more sanguine outlook given our already familiar relationship with technology in the workplace.[4]

In fact, as Peter Miscovich of the consulting firm JLL suggests, it is helpful to think of a more automated workplace in terms of advancement versus replacement. "The influx of sophisticated technologies will enable us to think of work in new and innovative ways," he argues, with robots doing the heavy lifting (like those annoying timesheets), allowing us to spend our time more productively and creatively. Like now, robots of the future are likely to be best at time-consuming and repetitive tasks, with no machine capable of doing everything a human can or at least as well. "As machine co-workers grow increasingly competent, human-to-machine collaboration technologies will make organizations more intelligent and greatly improve overall human work performance to drive greater business value," Miscovich happily concludes.[5]

Future Trend 51: Automation

Decision-Making and Leadership Platform

Implications

A more automated world is on the horizon.

- Mechanization is a fundamental part of the evolution of technology.

Robots are the inevitable outcome of the intersection between man and machine.

- The stuff of science fiction is being made real.

There are real, understandable fears about a jobless future.

- What robots will be capable of remains largely unknown.

There is consensus that in any scenario the workplace will change dramatically with greater automation.

- People will need to stay at least one step ahead of robots.

Optimists view a more robotic future as a good thing.

- Technology will continue to serve man rather than the other way around.

Humans are likely to work alongside robots in a collaborative, complementary manner.

- It will be a more advanced form of how we currently use computers and other digital technologies.

Opportunities

Anticipate a more automated workplace.

- All organizations will continue to be affected by ever-advancing technology.

Think of ways in which robots can be beneficial in your industry.

- Best-case-scenario: useful tools that help you do your job better.

Consider ways in which robots can negatively impact your industry.

- Worst-case-scenario: machines that make your business obsolete.

(continued)

Future Trend 51 (*continued*)

Embrace automation that helps people be more productive and creative.

- Let robots do the grunt work.

Future-proof your company now.

- Require employees to acquire new skill sets so that they can keep their jobs.

Adopt human-to-machine collaboration technologies that make your business more efficient and smarter.

- Look to automation as a continuation of the digital revolution versus the rise of the robots.

Future Trend 52: Biometrics

"It used to be that biometric technology was something that you only saw top-secret government agencies use in Hollywood flicks," Larry Alton wrote for ITProPortal.com in 2017, amazed as anyone that now the application was "available to the masses." In tech talk, biometrics are "the measurement and statistical analysis of physical and behavioural human characteristics which compares these measurements and characteristics with previously registered data to identify a person," according to industry expert Mehedi Hassan, a fancy way of saying that it determines whether someone really is who he or she purports to be. There are about eight billion people on the planet but each individual's fingerprints, palms, irises, faces, and even gait are somehow unique, making biometrics the most reliable means of identification.[6]

While indeed available to the masses—an iPhone 6 or later has Touch ID, Apple's biometric fingerprint identity sensor—many governments and corporations in information-sensitive industries such as health care and finance rely on the technology as the first wall of security. Now about a $10 billion business, biometrics is forecast to triple by 2022, a sign of the greater steps organizations are taking to protect their assets. The field is changing fast as technology improves, with new kinds of applications found continually. Healthcare professionals use mobile or portable devices in granting access to medical records, as does the Iraqi border control in determining who gets into that country. Clocking in and out at work may have been state-of-the-art technology in Henry Ford's day, but now more companies are using biometrics to examine employees' fingers, faces, and eyes when they arrive and depart in order to know how much time they put in.[7]

The range of ways that biometrics are currently being used suggests that the technology will become ubiquitous over the course of the next decade. The PIN-based system of authentication at ATMs will soon disappear, replaced by much more secure biometrics. (Turns out a lot of us use the same four numbers.) Retailers are rapidly adopting the technology to reduce credit card fraud, hacking into accounts, and identify theft. E-tailers too will swap out numerical or question-and-answer-based passwords for facial and voice recognition biometrics. (Thank goodness I will no longer have to remember some combination of the name of my childhood pet, my mother's birthplace, and the street on which I lived during the Carter administration.) Even your car (or personal flying device) will likely use biometrics before allowing you to drive it. Jaguar Land Rover is one automaker testing the technology to ensure the intended driver looks and walks like the registered owner and is not under the influence.[8]

Spend a few minutes thinking about it and one can imagine how biometrics will be used against the backdrop of other Future Trends. With geopolitical instability and anti-immigration sentiment showing no signs of reversing, expect fingerprint identification to become routine before traveling internationally or getting on any airplane. The transition from government to e-government will also make biometrics business as usual. "The use of biometrics will enable eGovernment processes to reliably identify citizens and safeguard the integrity of sensitive data stored in information systems," observed Danny Thakkar, co-founder of Bayometric, with reducing e-voter fraud another application coming our way. Finally, as the Internet of Things becomes a reality, biometrics will be used to authenticate the genuine identity of users, something of critical importance as machines increasingly talk with each other.[9]

Future Trend 52: Biometrics

Decision-Making and Leadership Platform

Implications

Biometrics are an increasing part of everyday life.

- They are part of the greater need for security in a digital world.

Unique physical characteristics are displacing older methods of identification such as a driver's license.

- There is a constant technological battle between the good and bad guys.

(continued)

Future Trend 52 (*continued*)

It is likely that governments and corporations will store each individual's biometric code.

- Even social security numbers will be retired.

Privacy issues are at stake but clearly the biometric train has already left the station.

- "Privacy" itself will become an archaic concept.

An exponential leap in biometrics will take place when devices intercommunicate.

- Fingerprint, voice, and facial identity will be required to do just about anything and get in or out of anywhere.

Parallel scientific Future Trends will bump into biometrics.

- Genomics and transhumanism will make one's physical identity not so clear-cut.

Opportunities

Integrate biometrics into your organization.

- They are the best way to secure resources in an increasingly dangerous world.

Apply biometric technology for the public good.

- Ultimate goal: a safer and more secure world in which the interests of individuals and organizations are protected.

Come up with interesting twists on biometric technology unique to your industry.

- Can brand experience be somehow personalized based on consumers' individual physical attributes?

Use advanced biometrics as a means to display corporate leadership and innovation.

- Make them an alternative means of differentiation in highly competitive categories.

(*continued*)

Future Trend 52 (*continued*)

Find creative ways to make biometrics less draconian.

- Example: an art installation using fingerprint, voice, or gait recognition.

Think of biometrics as yet another agent of individualism and omnicul-turalism.

- Geographically and socially defined borders are eroding.

Future Trend 53: Convergence

"Connectivity is pushing convergence," states Frost & Sullivan, making a strong case that industries, products, and technologies are becoming increasingly intertwined as devices and people link up. The research company is a big believer in the symbiotic relationship between connectivity and convergence, telling its clients that it is in their best interests to leverage what it considers to be a megatrend. "New technologies will enable multiple innovative applications that will change the way we live, communicate and conduct business, creating a connected world in the future," the company advises, astutely understanding the power of convergence and how it will shape our future.[10]

One can see how the leading edge of business is a strategic mash-up of industries, products, and technologies. The space industry is hooking up with the solar industry to produce space-based solar power, for example, while makers of automobiles are looking to unmanned technology to develop autonomous cars. Building technologies, meanwhile, are being matched up with smart automation to create smart home hubs, another example of the synergies to be gained when connectivity leads to convergence. Convergence is a principal means by which players in one industry can enter entirely new markets, Frost & Sullivan shows. Google has spawned a line of Nest home products by brainstorming how its technology can be applied in different ways, and Amazon has introduced Dash and Fire TV by doing the same. Facebook too has used convergence to expand its business beyond that of a social media platform, spinning off the Oculus virtual reality system and its Connectivity Labs aimed to make Internet access affordable to people everywhere.[11]

One doesn't have to be a Google, Amazon, or Facebook to take advantage of convergence, however. Even a mom-and-pop operation can forge new partnerships, after all, and sometimes this is the most direct route to growth. As well, cross-pollination across product categories or entire industries is entirely consistent with consumers' preference for technological compatibility and congruence. "Customers no longer are interested in silo based apps or services," explains Archana Amarnath, global director of the Visionary Innovation Group at Frost & Sullivan, thinking they "demand holistic, end-to end solutions of their connected life." To that end, it's entirely reasonable for a player in health care to team up with one in energy or a company in the security sector to partner with one in consumer goods, this convergence of seemingly strange bedfellows making for some very interesting products and services.[12]

What's perhaps most intriguing about the convergence resulting from technological connectivity is the erosion of borders among home, work, and community. Each of those environments has traditionally represented a distinct entity in market terms, but that is fast changing as more forward-thinking companies jump over the logistical boundaries that have long separated them. In telecom, for example, it is no longer anathema to blend platforms originally dedicated to residential, corporate, or municipal markets; consumers just want good service, and don't care where it comes from. The result of this kind of convergence is often a more intelligent and integrated product or service and greater consumer choice, explaining why it's becoming a more popular business model. "Connectivity and convergence will have a massive impact on business, society and personal lives," Frost & Sullivan concludes, envisioning "new solutions, new customers, and new partnerships and competition" in the marketplace of the future.[13]

Future Trend 53: Convergence

Decision-Making and Leadership Platform

Implications
Technology is breeding new kinds of connections in business.

- They are mutually beneficial, synergistic alliances.

Convergence in various forms is a key theme across society.

- There is unprecedented opportunity to forge relationships with other people and organizations.

New businesses are being founded by borrowing technologies, systems, and ideas from other industries.

- Lateral or horizontal thinking is a big plus.

(continued)

Future Trend 53 (*continued*)

The traditional lines that have separated industries and product categories are becoming less rigid.

- Business is now a more fluid and permeable arena.

Consumers are open to industry and category crossovers and fusions.

- Corporate territorialism is not at all relevant.

The laissez-faire marketplace is driving companies to offer consumers more choices.

- Convergence is encouraging a hybrid-based economy.

Opportunities
Leverage the direct relationship between connectivity and convergence.

- New solutions, new customers, and new partnerships and competition are attainable.

Seek out opportunistic convergences.

- Choose industries, products, and technologies that offer potential synergies.

Take a horizontal versus vertical view of the marketplace.

- Lateral thinking reveals a broader range of opportunities.

Get to know industry "cousins" who share some business interests while not being directly competitive.

- The best partnerships are a combination of commonality and difference.

Lift ideas from seemingly unrelated product and service categories.

- "Innovation" is often a result of reconceiving and repackaging versus pure originality.

Challenge consumers' expectations and preconceptions.

- The postindustrial marketplace is receptive to disruptive strategies and tactics.

Future Trend 54: Intelligence

What is the common denominator of many if not most emerging technologies? Smartness or intelligence (i.e., the ability of machines to not just process information but to make decisions and "think" on their own). "In the future, data driven 'things' and smart algorithms will start making independent decisions," notes Dutch futurist Richard van Hooijdonk, seeing the accelerating autonomy of the nonhuman universe as something that will reshape the contours of everyday life. Indeed, some form of intelligence serves as the primary currency of many applied technologies such as drones, health devices, appliances, security systems, and, very soon, self-driving automobiles. Computer-based artificial intelligence mimics that of humans by automating such abilities to see, hear, speak, and learn, the latter increasingly in real time. "In ten years, we will no longer be able to tell the difference between certain types of robots and humans," says van Hooijdonk, the divide between man and machine getting ever-narrower.[14]

So how does one make a machine intelligent? Data, and the more the better. "Big data is becoming an increasingly important link in every possible aspect of our lives," van Hooijdonk continues, these collected pieces of information the key to "start, prevent, reduce and predict anything and everything." There are already more such nuggets than the number of stars in the known universe, and, by 2020, it's estimated that we will have roughly forty-four zettabytes (or forty-four trillion gigabytes) of them. Such unfathomable quantities of data are not just the means by which to solve complex problems but offer a greater likelihood of accurately predicting future scenarios, as good as any measure of intelligence.[15]

To see the future of artificial intelligence and machine learning, one need not look further than IBM's Cognitive Horizons Network. The network is "a consortium of the world's leading universities committed to working with IBM to accelerate development of important technologies needed to fulfill the promise of cognitive computing," the company explains, with hundreds of scientists currently pursuing research that may help solve some of our biggest problems. Not just scientists and engineers were chosen to be a part of the network but academics in other fields such as philosophy, sociology, psychology, and law, consistent with the fact that intelligent technology is a holistic enterprise that will affect virtually all aspects of society. IBM is taking a wide swath with its network, from digging deep into raw data to constructing the frameworks required to take advantage of what the company calls "a truly digital world."[16]

The range of projects within IBM's Cognitive Horizons Network points to how smart machines—yes, like souped-up versions of the company's famous computer Watson—will likely be used in the future. A team at MIT, for example, is working on video comprehension (i.e., the ability for machines to comprehend visual data and, using that information, predict what may happen next in real time). Problem solving and decision making by teams of humans and computers is the focus at RPI, while folks at the University of Michigan are working on conversational technologies (i.e., how people and machines can better communicate). And at the University of Maryland, cognitive cybersecurity is the priority, in which the online universe is scanned to determine potential threats. Intelligent machines have a long way to go (the average current robot is about as smart as a dog), but recall that the 2011 version of Watson beat champion Ken Jennings handily in *Jeopardy!*—a sign of much bigger things to come.[17]

Future Trend 54: Intelligence

Decision-Making and Leadership Platform

Implications

Machines are becoming more intelligent or smarter.

- They are increasingly capable of simulating humans' abilities to think and act.

The end goal of artificial intelligence and machine learning is independent decision making and problem solving.

- Current research is dedicated to enabling deduction and prediction.

Robots and people are becoming more similar.

- Machines are increasingly human-like while humans are increasingly machine-like.

Data and algorithms are the basis for technological intelligence.

- They replicate the neural connections of the brain.

Much time and money are being spent to determine how to make machines do more things and do them better.

- It is one of the primary initiatives of contemporary science and technology.

(continued)

Future Trend 54 (*continued*)

A shotgun approach is being used to push machine intelligence.

- It is in a relatively early stage of research with many potential applications.

Opportunities

Seed the concept of intelligence throughout your organization.

- Technology is propelling the value and worth of smartness of all kinds.

Take a macro view of intelligence.

- There are many different paths to good decision making and problem solving.

Invest in intelligent technology.

- Smart machines will inevitable play a larger role in both our professional and personal lives.

Form your own mini-initiative based on technological cognition.

- Create a specific application for your company.

Develop the first smart "something" in your industry.

- Create a product or service that is deemed somehow intelligent.

Contribute to the conversation surrounding the rise of intelligent machines capable of thinking on their own.

- At what point does technology impede versus facilitate humanity?

Future Trend 55: Mobility

When you think about it, how we've moved from one place to another hasn't really changed much over the past century. Technology has made modes of transportation faster and more comfortable, of course, but the automobiles, airplanes, trains, ships, and even bicycles of today are not much different in terms of functionality or even design than those used during World War I. (Compare that to communication, where the ways in which we exchange information now are a world apart from the methods we used even as recently as the 1980s.) If there has been any major leap in mobility in recent years it is without doubt the electric car, a technological advance that promises to permanently retire the environmental disaster that is the combustion engine.

Today, however, we are on the brink of a technological revolution in what people in the field like to call our "mobility ecosystem." "Frictionless, automated, personalized travel on demand—that's the dream of the future of mobility," muse Corwin, Jameson, Pankratz, and Willigmann of Deloitte, convinced that "the extended auto ecosystem's various elements are co-alescing to realize that dream sooner than expected." Individually owned, driver-operated vehicles will in the not-so-distant-future become part of transportation history, the giant business consultancy and advisory company believes after talking with top executives, elected officials, and industry experts. In their place will come a system predicated on driverless vehicles and shared mobility, a model much more consistent with the evolution of smarter, greener, and safer cities. A few states are already laying the regula-tory foundation for this kind of future mobility ecosystem, thinking that it could not just lead to a healthier, more efficient urban environment but also spur economic growth by attracting more people and businesses.[18]

Much is being made of the autonomous vehicle, of course, with GM, Ford, and Daimler just a few automobile companies working fast to bring it to the marketplace. Alongside the self-driving car, however, are a host of other tech-nologies that will create the mobility ecosystem of the future. Electric vehicles, carsharing, a banning of street parking, smart traffic signals, and improvements in intermodal or mixed-mode passenger transport (e.g., park-and-ride or rail links) are also remaking the urban transportation grid as we know it.[19]

But as self-driving cars become a reality, automakers are partnering with entertainment and content marketers to fill what will likely be a consider-able amount of time as passengers wait to get to their destinations. "'Experi-ence enablers'—content providers, in-vehicle service providers, data and analytics companies, advertisers, entertainment equipment providers, and social media companies—will clamor to make the in-transit experience whatever we want it to be," Deloitte predicts, with time spent in automo-biles to be "relaxing, productive, or entertaining." Volvo has hooked up with Netflix to allow commuters to enjoy streaming video while their self-driven cars cruise down the road, for example, the beginning of what may turn automobiles into mobile home theaters. In fact, Ford has already patented an "Autonomous Vehicle Entertainment System," in which the whole wind-shield transforms into a video screen. Passengers (versus drivers) will be able to use not just their eyes for other purposes but their hands as well, suggesting that web browsing will be a common activity in the cabins of future cars. The possibilities for reimagining what was arguably the most important invention of all time—the automobile—are nearly endless, as are the prospects for how we move from Point A to Point B.[20]

Future Trend 55: Mobility

Decision-Making and Leadership Platform

Implications
How we move from one place to another is in flux.

- Smart technologies are ushering in a new age of mobility.

Electric cars are the beginnings of the transportation revolution.

- The time is right for that technology after it was suppressed by the oil industry and others in the 1990s.

A shift in attitudes is encouraging the development of a new kind of mobility ecosystem.

- Many are receptive to alternatives to driving their own cars at least part of the time.

Driverless vehicles, carsharing, and smarter streetscapes represent the new model of mobility.

- It is the biggest change in transportation since the invention of the automobile.

Smart technologies and automation are enabling a wholesale shift in how we get around.

- It is another example of machines displacing humans.

Vehicles will eventually morph into self-contained technology centers.

- Eyes and hands will be freed up for other activities.

Opportunities
Brace yourself for the new mobility ecosystem.

- How will the revolution in transportation affect you and your organization?

(*continued*)

Future Trend 55 (*continued*)

Integrate key deliverables of this new system into your own business.

- Think safety, greenness, convenience, efficiency.

Look to the emerging model of mobility as the kind of breakthrough about which many industries dream.

- What scenario would represent an equivalent leap in innovation in your product or service category?

Leverage the cultural shift toward sharing versus owning.

- What else can be transformed into a collective versus possessive model?

Use local, regional, and federal governments to identify potential opportunities.

- Public interests are often the drivers of private initiatives.

Make your brand experience more relaxing, productive, or entertaining.

- These are the key consumer benefits of our time and place.

Future Trend 56: Predictives

"It's tough to make predictions, especially about the future," goes yet another pithy Yogi Berra phrase, its head-scratching convolution matched only by its essential truth. Consistently predicting the future is actually not just tough but impossible, any real futurist will tell you, but technology is turning the art of prediction into more of a science. Many organizations are in fact determining what will likely happen next through predictive analytics, a field that is fast gaining popularity. Ascertaining customer buying behavior, digital ad placement, and even a sales forecast are examples of predictive analytics, although the area of statistics is evolving into a much more sophisticated practice as more companies acquire Big Data.[21] What I call predictives as a whole will make great advancements in the future, I believe, as machines (and hopefully humans) become more intelligent.

How do predictive analysts do the voodoo that they do? First, quants sort as much historical and transactional data as possible into buckets, with certain relationships or patterns soon becoming apparent. These patterns are viewed as potential risks and opportunities, and are given scores or weights that represent the quantitative likelihood of happening in the future. Statistical analysis and modeling come next, leading to a body of useful information, a set of conclusions, and an action plan. It sounds complicated—because it is—but boiled down, predictive analytics is about answering three basic questions: What happened and why? What is happening now? What is going to happen in the future? Predictive analytics allows organizations to become proactive versus reactive, this alone making it a worthwhile endeavor.[22]

As Big Data gets bigger, the business applications of predictive analytics are growing. Customer relationship management (CRM) and cross selling are primary ways it is being used, understandably; past buying behavior is often a good predictor of future buying behavior. Health care is another major application, with predictive analytics helpful in determining which people are likely to develop long-term medical conditions such as asthma and diabetes. Some collection agencies use predictive analytics to identify the greatest chance of recovering a debt, and credit card companies use it to detect fraud and identity theft. Finance people are increasingly looking to predictive analytics for portfolio management, and a host of other industries, including oil and gas, pharmaceuticals, travel, retail, telecommunications, banking, and insurance are also using customized or off-the-shelf software to anticipate future events.[23]

Because success in business can be seen as being in the right place at the right time with the right ideas, it can easily be seen why any kind of reliable predictor of the future will itself be much sought after. "More and more organizations are turning to predictive analytics to increase their bottom line and competitive advantage," explains SAS, one of the key players in the industry, citing more and more kinds of data, ever-rising computer power, user-friendly software, and greater receptivity toward quantitative-based consumer insight as the reasons for the fast growth of the field.[24] But perhaps the biggest reason more managers are putting predictive analytics in their tool kit is the old diaper-and-beer story. Men who shopped for diapers were also most likely to be buying beer, a data-mining retailer reportedly found, reason enough to move the two product categories closer together in stores to increase sales of each. The story has only some basis in truth, but still serves as a key selling tool for the power of predictives.[25]

Future Trend 56: Predictives
Decision-Making and Leadership Platform

Implications
Predicting the future is getting somewhat easier.

- The impossible is becoming more possible.

The art of prediction is evolving into a science.

- Advanced information technology enables a new era of data-gathering and analysis.

A golden age of futurism beckons.

- It is the quantitative equivalent to the fantastical version of the late nineteenth century.

More businesses are embracing predictive analytics.

- It is a helpful tool for decision making.

Huge volumes of information about past and present behavior indicate future behavior.

- The sheer amount of data makes prediction more reliable.

The bottom line of predictive analytics is: proactivity versus reactivity.

- A wait-and-see approach is often too little too late.

Opportunities
Improve your ability to predict the future.

- Past and present behavior are an increasingly reliable indicator of what will happen next.

Break down prediction into its essentials.

- What happened, what is happening, what will happen?

Use predictive analytics as an alternative avenue of consumer insight.

- It is a form of quantitative research that goes beyond surveys and questionnaires.

(continued)

Future Trend 56 (*continued*)

Trade data with companies in other industries.

- It is a cost-effective means of gaining ability to do predictive analytics.

Develop alternative forms of prediction.

- Choose research methods uniquely suited to your industry or company that point to future behavior.

Adopt a proactive versus reactive philosophy through your organization.

- Reward employees for the ability to think one (or two) steps ahead.

Future Trend 57: Quantum

In the television show *Quantum Leap* that ran on NBC between 1989 and 1993, lead character physicist Sam Beckett finds himself stuck in the past when a time travel experiment goes awry. Over the course of five seasons and ninety-seven episodes, Beckett tries to return to the present (the late twentieth century) by "leaping from life to life," as the opening narration went, specifically by correcting wrongs of the past. Beckett is assisted by the hologram of his friend Admiral Al Calavicci, who keeps track of Beckett's whereabouts from the present.[26]

Leaping through time has yet to be achieved, but we can be very excited about approaching quantum-based technology. Quantum computing, in which calculations would be performed at the subatomic level, has yet to be developed, but many experts, including Bill Gates, believe it may very well be within the next decade. As powerful as they are, contemporary computers still process information using a series of zeros and ones; a quantum computer would be far more powerful and fast by allowing those bytes to work at the same time instead of sequentially. IBM, Google, Hewlett-Packard, Microsoft, and others are working on quantum technology, knowing that it could represent the next big thing in computing.[27] Why the big deal? "Quantum computers will solve problems that conventional computers never could," Jeremy O'Brien wrote for *Financial Times* in 2017, seeing the technology as being potentially able to find solutions for the critical challenges such as energy, health care, and climate change. "Many of the problems that seem so suited to computing are still incredibly hard, and our conventional computers are not only currently inadequate but will forever remain so," he brooded.[28]

Given the diminishing returns of our current computers, the potential arrival of quantum would thus be perfect timing. "The good news is that a solution is at hand," O'Brien continued, with quantum serving as "a drastically different approach to computing that is profound both in terms of the fundamental laws of physics it exploits, and the transformations it will bring about in our lives, society and economy."[29] Kelly Dickerson of businessinsider.com is equally charged up about the future of quantum. In her article "7 Awesome Ways Quantum Computers Will Change the World," Dickerson explains that the sci-fiesque concept of tens of millions of parallel realities could possibly "revolutionize entire industries." A quantum computer would be much more like a human brain than a conventional computer, making its development yet another technological bridge between man and machine.[30]

What might these seemingly magical devices be able do? Super accurate weather forecasting to save lives, for one thing, as well as superior climate modeling so we can better understand the relationship between humans and the environment. Determining which drugs will be most effective for a particular patient would be another application, and quantum technology would mesh perfectly with the planned mobility ecosystem of the future through intelligent traffic control both on the road and in the air. Not surprisingly, the military would make full use of the technology for defense purposes, and making online communication more secure through encryption would also be possible. Finally, quantum computing could advance space exploration by analyzing data faster than a speeding bullet, and the technology would dovetail nicely with the ongoing effort to make machines think and learn much like humans.[31] The prospect of quantum computing is indeed nothing short of awesome.

Future Trend 57: Quantum

Decision-Making and Leadership Platform

Implications
Current information technology is reaching its maximum capabilities.

- Moore's Law (the doubling of computer power every two years) is running out of steam.

An exponential leap in information technology is on the horizon.

- It will be much more than just standard incremental progress.

Quantum computing will likely change the landscape of technology.

- It will make today's computers seem like Tinker Toys.

(continued)

Future Trend 57 (*continued*)

There is a consensus that quantum computing can lead to great things if it can be developed successfully.

- It will be an extension of our persistent faith and trust in technology.

Some of the smartest people in the room are racing to make quantum technology a reality.

- A deep understanding of the complexities of physics is required.

Big rewards await the first developers of quantum.

- All kinds of potential applications in all kinds of industries can be realized.

Opportunities
Seek out potential quantum leaps in your industry.

- How can you reinvent a product or service by taking a drastically different approach?

Find solutions to the same critical challenges that quantum computing will address.

- Examples are energy, health care, climate change, etc.

Explore the fertile territory located between man and machine.

- What other ways can technology enable human-like intelligence?

Focus on the key deliverables of quantum computing in your own business.

- They include greater accuracy, efficiency, security.

Reach for the secret sauce of quantum computing.

- Achieve the ability to solve multiple problems at the same time.

Add a physicist to your technology team.

- Breakthrough discoveries reside in the study of matter and motion through space and time.

Future Trend 58: Wearables

Like most first waves of technology, wearables (notably FitBit) were over-priced, clunky, and underperforming. (Remember those walkie-talkie-like mobile phones of the 1980s?) Future generations of wearables—electronics that can be worn on the body—will resemble those early products in name only, and ultimately become a standard feature on human bodies. Wearables will dramatically shrink in size, for one thing, so much so that they will look and feel as if they are part of our physical selves. "Between conductive fabrics or sensor-clad smart garments," Jen Quinlan of the gesture recognition company Rithmio observed, "wearables will intertwine so closely with fashion we won't be able to distinguish them apart." Clothing and accessories that provide users with a variety of biometric data are already here, suggesting that subsequent versions of wearables will offer as much or more information on bodily status and cognitive performance as a medical checkup.[32]

Current off-the-rack, one-size-fits-all wearable tech will also soon go the way of the any-color-as-long-as-it's-black Model T. Personalized wearables are coming, designed and programmed for individuals' unique bodies (and minds, given that they will be able to read not just brain activity but thought patterns). Although batteries will also shrink in size and power, wearables will increasingly rely on the body's own forms of energy (heat and kinet-ics, notably) as a power source. The range of data provided will extend far beyond the number of steps walked or one's heart rate, meanwhile, offering not only past and present physical and cognitive metrics but what kind of activities the body and mind are best equipped for at any given time.[33]

Even the term wearables will go away as the technology improves and be-comes fully integrated into the body's ecosystem. Customized sets of external and internal sensors will replace the fashion and accessory model, with these microdevices continually gathering data that are then connected to some kind of grid. "Technologists are working on ways to derive meaning from multiple sensors on the body at one time, to give a person a holistic view of how her body is moving or performing," according to Quinlan, with that information perhaps to be used to determine optimal and less-than-optimal external environments or physical spaces to occupy. Sentient wearables, in which one's set of sensors can express thoughts or maybe even feelings, will represent an advanced generation of the technology (much like that in the 2013 film Her). And like people, wearables will one day be able to change and evolve over time, deepening the relationship between man and machine.[34]

In the near term, however, wearables are likely to stay close to their ori-gins as monitors of health and fitness. "I see wearables increasing proactive healthcare measures by creating efficiencies in how we monitor our own health, and how we communicate our health status to healthcare providers," stated Angela McIntyre, research director at Gartner, this advance information on a person's medical status good for the wearer, physicians, and insurance companies. Detecting a coronary incident or stroke before it happens is one example of how wearables can serve as vital tools to save lives and money. Biosensory patches are currently providing caregivers with valuable clues related to a patient's condition, just the beginnings of what will be a new branch of medicine dedicated to electronic diagnostics.[35] The future of wearables is a promising one as innovators conceive new ways in which they can contribute to the well-being of society.

Future Trend 58: Wearables

Decision-Making and Leadership Platform

Implications
Wearable technology is evolving quickly.

- It is related to biometrics, predictives, and other Future Trends.

Nanotechnology and wearables will eventually meet head-on.

- Bodies and devices are becoming increasingly integrated and seamless.

Everyone's respective set of wearables will be somehow different.

- They will be custom-designed and -engineered based on each individual's unique physical chemistry.

Predictive abilities will become wearables' most valuable asset.

- They will indicate what a person should do and not do based on current vital signs and other health-related measurements.

Sensors will open a new world of possibilities for wearables.

- They will make connections with other devices and the next generation of the Internet.

Future wearables will offer two-way communication.

- They will enable the humanization of technology and the technologicalization of humans.

(continued)

Future Trend 58 (*continued*)

Opportunities
Get ready for the mainstreaming of wearables.

- Many if not most of us will have some kind of device on or in our body in the next decade or two.

Glom onto the growing interest in equipping ourselves with smart gear.

- How can your product or service tie in to wearables as they evolve?

Partner with a tech company in the biosensory space.

- Determine the potential effects of your brands on a consumer's body chemistry.

Apply the key benefits of wearables to your business.

- Get real-time information on bodily status and cognitive performance.

Mine wearables' current primary reason for being: maintaining or improving one's health and/or fitness.

- They have almost universal appeal, especially among the aging population.

Tap into the predictive abilities of wearables.

- Detect potential problems before they happen.

Future Trend 59: Virtuality

"Which world is real?" asks Richard van Hooijdonk, the Dutch futurist, the answer being "with virtual reality it will be hard to tell." Virtual and augmented reality (VR and AR) technology is exploding, with new applications continually being found for each. Thankfully, the technology promises to go far beyond gaming and entertainment, with simulated realities offering all kinds of business opportunities and benefits to society. Innovative uses of VR and AR are being found in education, emergency management, therapy, urban planning, and many more fields, making what I call "virtuality" one of the key themes of the future.[36]

Emerging technologies related to the Internet of Things (IoT), in which digital devices are connected to each other, are running parallel with advancements in virtuality, and creating powerful synergies that are bound to make "reality" a more subjective experience. Some in the tech sector are calling this mash-up of VR/AR and IoT "mixed reality" or MR, something that will find particular use in the business world. "With MR, the virtual and real worlds come together to create new environments in which both digital and physical objects—and their data—can coexist and interact with one another," Nelson Kunkel and Steve Soechtig of Deloitte explain, the result being a "shift in engagement patterns that allows more natural and behavioral interfaces." In these immersive virtual universes or "sandboxes," information can be exchanged between people in different locations in a far more "real" way than previously possible. Mixed-reality scenarios can also be used in training and operations, and by enabling team members scattered around the world to think and act as if they were in the same room.[37]

For marketers, virtuality may represent a dream come true by making remote shopping a much more realistic experience. Online shoppers will be able to not just look at a product on their computer screens but "hold" and even "use" it much like they would in the real world. At the same time, marketers will get instant feedback about how consumers literally feel about their brand. As well, the physical landscape of a retail store can be re-created online through virtuality, with shoppers picking out items and then trying them on in dressing rooms. Those in the travel and hospitality industry should be particularly excited about the possibilities of virtuality. Consumers will be able to check out a hotel and room before making a reservation by perceiving that they are really there, or perhaps preview a destination prior to choosing where to go on vacation. In short, virtuality represents an entirely new way for marketers to present their product or service and a revolutionary tool for businesses of all kinds. "If done correctly, mixed reality may open floodgates for transforming how tomorrow's enterprises are built and operated," Kunkel and Soechtig observe, the postindustrial economy getting a much-needed overhaul through the magic of technology.[38]

Of course, virtuality has potential applications far beyond the world of commerce. Learning will certainly be transformed by immersive technologies, in the process expanding the boundaries of education. Training for careers such as social work and psychology could be helped immensely through immersive technologies, for example, with students exposed to real-world situations before entering their respective fields.[39] Virtual town hall meetings can be created across the country (and world), allowing millions of citizens to come together to demonstrate democracy in action. The possibilities of virtuality are, in a word, limitless.

Future Trend 59: Virtuality

Decision-Making and Leadership Platform

Implications
The real and unreal worlds are colliding.

- A new universe of mixed reality or virtuality is being created.

The interest in immersive experiences is moving far beyond that of gaming and entertainment as their potential becomes clear.

- The underlying supposition is that the mind believes what one's senses tell it to believe.

Internal operations are leading the way for virtuality in business settings.

- This supplies the means to make a company run smoother and smarter.

Marketing is the next major application of virtuality.

- It meshes perfectly with the rise of e-commerce.

The basic infrastructure of society—education, government, transportation, etc.—is another looming platform for virtuality.

- Transformative possibilities await if the technology is used properly.

The codes of social interaction will be rewritten as virtuality gains traction.

- Relationships with simulated people will be considered perfectly legitimate.

Opportunities
Stir up the real and unreal.

- There is great interest in experiencing alternative realities.

Identify the virtual killer app for your industry or product category.

- How can an immersive experience change (and improve) the way things are done normally?

Create virtual scenarios that make consumers feel good.

- Pleasure, contentment, and happiness are users' ultimate goal.

(*continued*)

Future Trend 59 (*continued*)

Use pop-up kiosks to allow consumers to virtually experience your product or service.

- It is the twenty-first-century version of sampling.

Stake out territory in emerging areas of virtuality.

- These include mental and physical therapy, learning, training, education, the arts, sports, entertainment, etc.

Match organizational assets with potential applications of virtuality.

- How can your corporate and/or brand values be translated into virtual terms?

Future Trend 60: Singularity

"The singularity is near," went the title of Ray Kurzweil's landmark 2005 book that rocked the world by pronouncing that humans would be able to move beyond their biological makeup in the not-so-distant future. People and technology will merge in 2045, the inventor and futurist claimed, a literally life-changing event resulting from exponentially advanced artificial intelligence. Humans, or whatever we would be called, would comprise a new and different kind of species, not an easy idea to wrap one's head around, especially since it will supposedly take place in many of our lifetimes. The singularity is "an era in which our intelligence will become increasingly nonbiological and trillions of times more powerful than it is today," Kurzweil proposed, with technological change leading to "the dawning of a new civilization that will enable us to transcend our biological limitations and amplify our creativity."[40]

Even if one finds it tough to believe that the singularity is coming in less than three decades, it seems clear that some kind of fusion between humans and machines is inevitable at some point. A fair number of the Future Trends presented here have at least something to do with the intersection of the body and technology, suggesting that we may indeed be heading toward a "post-human" age. Whether it's through artificial intelligence, "self-aware" computer networks, a super-advanced human-computer linking device, or some kind of giant stride in biology, as Vernor Vinge has proposed, the notion of technological superiority has moved beyond science fiction. Still, the reality of machines not just acting and making decisions on their own but creating improved versions of themselves is to me about as scary a scenario as can be imagined.[41]

If Kurzweil is right (he is credited as being 86 percent right when predicting the future), the kinds of change in store for humanity are difficult to fathom. Artificial intelligence will match that of humans by 2029, he believes, triggering a wholesale shift in the way we go about our lives. Virtual reality will be so advanced that it will make going to a workplace unnecessary and, by the early 2030s, it will be possible to move human consciousness to any kind of digitally encoded device. With our bodies made superfluous, the content of our minds could be formatted into a brain scan, and then applied to any form imaginable. (I'm leaning toward that of a Porsche 911.) If that were not enough, that pesky problem of dying would be solved; our brains would be independent of our physical selves. "Kurzweil envisions a future that is exciting, daunting, and a little bit terrifying all at once," Patrick Caughill wrote for futurism.com, with only "time to tell if his impressive batting average will improve or if the future has other plans for humanity."[42]

Happily, most futurists (including myself) believe that it will take considerably longer for robots or their technological equivalent to start bossing people around. Many say the singularity will occur in the twenty-second century, giving us some breathing room for the change of changes to take place. Even Stephen Hawking and Alan Turing are disturbed by the prospect of humans not being the most intelligent organisms on the planet; each genius has recognized that at some point we would become subservient to machines, not unlike the storylines in a good number of sci-fi films. Even SpaceX founder Elon Musk, who is putting a lot of money into artificial intelligence, understands its long-term consequences.[43] Regardless of such concerns, the technological march toward singularity continues, making it perhaps more a matter of when than whether.

Future Trend 60: Singularity

Decision-Making and Leadership Platform

Implications

The prospect of machines ruling people is not a new idea.

- It has been a fear ever since the Industrial Revolution.

(continued)

Future Trend 60 (*continued*)

An army of robots will potentially wield power not with their strength but their intelligence.

- The possibility of smarter-than-human machines emerged in the 1950s.

Singularity is the logical consequence of exponentially rising machine intelligence.

- The artificial will eclipse the human at some unknown point in time.

A "post-humanity" stage of evolution is already in progress.

- Many different kinds of mechanical parts are increasingly being incorporated into our biology.

Many other human-machine interfaces are wrapped up in artificial intelligence.

- These include virtual reality, nanobots, etc.

It is hard to see an approaching singularity in positive terms.

- Replacing the humanity of humans with something else is simply too frightening an idea.

Opportunities
Plan for artificial intelligence to approach that of humans in our lifetimes.

- It will be the ultimate expression of our continual urge to build better and better machines.

Welcome any and all kinds of intelligence that make the world a better place.

- People have been accommodating machines in their everyday lives for at least half a millennium.

View machines as a form of empowerment until proven otherwise.

- There is no evidence yet of any machine independently serving nefarious ends.

(*continued*)

Future Trend 60 (*continued*)

Explore how artificial intelligence can be applied in your industry.

- How can your brands be made smarter?

Address the same kind of opportunity areas that artificial intelligence promises to.

- These include memory and other cognitive issues, medical diagnoses, financial trading, etc.

Be a voice of socially responsible artificial intelligence.

- Serve as a reminder that technology should serve human ends rather than the other way around.

Notes

Introduction

1. David Remnick, "Future Perfect," *New Yorker*, October 20–27, 1997, 215.

2. David A. Wilson, *The History of the Future* (Toronto: McArthur & Company, 2000), 12.

3. William A. Henry III, "Ready or Not, Here It Comes," *Time*, October 15, 1992, 34.

4. Thomas Griffith, "Obsessed by the Future," *Time*, September 3, 1979, 46.

5. Stefan Kanfer, "Is There Any Future in Futurism?" *Time*, May 17, 1976, 51.

6. David Rejeski and Robert L. Olson, "Has Futurism Failed?" *Wilson Quarterly*, Winter 2006, 14.

7. Lewis Lapham, "The Rage Against the Future," *Harper's*, November 1979, 21; James Poniewozik, "Why We're So Obsessed with 'Next,'" *Time*, September 8, 2003, 94.

8. Nassim Nicholas Taleb, *The Black Swan: The Impact of the Highly Improbable* (New York: Random House, 2007).

9. George F. Mechlin, "Seven Technologies for the Future," *USA Today*, January 1983, 62.

10. David Bouchier, "In the Fast Lane with Nostradamus," *New York Times*, December 31, 1995, LI12.

11. Isaac Asimov, "Life in 1990," *Science Digest*, August 1965, 63.

12. Lev Grossman, "Forward Thinking," *Time*, October 11, 2004, 58–59.

13. A. S. W. Rosenbach, "Old Almanacs and Prognostications," *Saturday Evening Post*, June 8, 1935, 10–11.

14. Fletcher Pratt, "What's the World Coming To?" *Saturday Review of Literature*, April 2, 1938, 3–4.

15. Pratt, "What's the World Coming To?"

16. Harry Harrison, "Introducing the Future: The Dawn of Science-Fiction Criticism," in *Histories of the Future: Studies in Fact, Fantasy and Science Fiction*, ed. Alan Sandison and Robert Dingley (New York: Palgrave, 2000), 6.

Chapter 1. Cultural Trends

1. Victoria Woollaston, "Think the 'Me Me Me Generation' is New? Think Again: Society Began Shifting Towards Individualism More Than a Century Ago," dailymail.co.uk, July 26, 2015.

2. Jay Ogilvy, "The Global Spread of Individualism," worldview.stratfor.com, October 14, 2015.

3. Moises Naim, *The End of Power: From Boardrooms to Battlefields and Churches to States, Why Being In Charge Isn't What It Used to Be* (New York: Basic, 2014), 58.

4. "Megatrend #4 Individualism," trend-monitor.com.uk, June 8, 2015.

5. Michael F. Haverluck, "Religion Fading, Secularism Increasingly Globally," onenewsnow.com, May 15, 2016.

6. "Are You Humanist?" americanhumanist.org.

7. Haverluck, "Religion Fading."

8. Haverluck, "Religion Fading"; Gabe Bullard, "The World's Newest Major Religion: No Religion," news.nationalgeographic.com, April 22, 2016; D. J. Tice, "While West Grows Secular, the World Gets Religion," startribune.com, April 15, 2016.

9. Haverluck, "Religion Fading."

10. "Are You Humanist?"

11. Haverluck, "Religion Fading."

12. Haverluck, "Religion Fading"; Bullard, "World's Newest Major Religion"; Tice, "While West Grows Secular."

13. Jerry A. Coyne, *Faith Versus Fact: Why Science and Religion Are Incompatible* (New York: Viking, 2015), 64.

14. Richard Dobbs, James Manyika, and Jonathan Woetzel, "The Four Global Forces Breaking All the Trends," mckinsey.com, April 2015.

15. Andy Beckett, "Accelerationism: How a Fringe Philosophy Predicted the Future We Live In," theguardian.com, June 5, 2017.

16. Wendy Broadgate, "The Great Acceleration," futureearth.org, January 16, 2015.

17. Beckett, "Accelerationism."

18. Robert Browning, "Andrea del Sarto," poetryfoundation.org.

19. Ludwig Mies van der Rohe, phrases.org.uk.

20. Lawrence R. Samuel, *The American Way of Life: A Cultural History* (London: Fairleigh Dickinson University Press, 2017), 105.

21. "Less is More—the Minimalism," focusingfuture.com.

22. Neil Howe, "When Less is More," forbes.com, October 14, 2016.

23. Barry Schwartz, *The Paradox of Choice: Why More is Less* (New York: Harper-Collins, 2004).

24. Howe, "When Less is More."

25. Joseph Pine and James Gilmore, *The Experience Economy: Work is Theater & Every Business a Stage* (Cambridge, MA: Harvard Business School Press, 1999).

26. James Wallman, "Spend Less on Stuff, More on Experiences," theguardian.com, May 25, 2017.

27. Wallman, "Spend Less on Stuff."

28. "The Secret to Happiness? Spend Money on Experiences, Not Things," forbes.com, March 3, 2016.

29. Brian Schultz, "Not Just Millennials: Consumers Want Experiences, Not Things," adage.com, August 18, 2015.

30. Jonathan Bacon, "Millennials Look for Experiences Over Possessions," marketingweek.com, February 18, 2015.

31. Schultz, "Not Just Millennials."

32. Lindsey Lukacs, "Androgynous Clothing Blurs the Lines Between Male and Female Fashion," thepostathens.com, February 8, 2017.

33. Lukacs, "Androgynous Clothing Blurs the Lines."

34. Molly Hannelly, "Trend Report: Androgyny," moodfabrics.com, June 28, 2017.

35. Ellen Thomas, "Makeup for Men: Fad or Future?" wwd.com, October 19, 2016.

36. Lisa Capretto, "How Parents Can Start to Dismantle Traditional Gender Roles for Their Kids," huffingtonpost.com, July 22, 2016.

37. Ivana Milojevic, "Gender Issues: Futures and Implications for Global Humanity," metafuture.com.

38. Max Daly, "The Future of Drugs According to VICE," vice.com, January 13, 2015.

39. Daly, "The Future of Drugs."

40. Daly, "The Future of Drugs."

41. Zach Weissmueller and Alex Manning, "Psychedelic Drugs: The Future of Mental Health," reason.com, May 12, 2017.

42. Lawrence R. Samuel, *Boomers 3.0: Marketing to Baby Boomers in Their Third Act of Life* (Santa Barbara, CA: Praeger, 2017), 6–7.

43. Samuel, *Boomers 3.0*, 7.

44. Samuel, *Boomers 3.0*, 7–8.

45. Samuel, *Boomers 3.0*, 8.

46. Samuel, *Boomers 3.0*, 84–85.

47. wisdomresearch.org.

48. wisdomresearch.org.

49. wisdomresearch.org.

50. Saul McLeod, "Maslow's Hierarchy of Needs," simplypsychology.org, 2016.

51. Samuel, *Boomers 3.0*, 87.

52. Quoted in Leslie Hart, "The Betterment Trend: Pursuing Wellbeing," kitchen-bathdesign.com, June 27, 2016.

53. Melissa Thompson, "Self-Actualization Is the New Carrot Everyone Is Chasing," newsblaze.com, July 23, 2016.

Chapter 2. Economic Trends

1. C. R., "When Did Globalisation Start?" *Economist*, September 23, 2013.

2. Kimberly Amadeo, "Deregulation Pros, Cons, and Examples," thebalance.com, January 26, 2017.

3. Amadeo, "Deregulation Pros, Cons, and Examples."

4. Amadeo, "Deregulation Pros, Cons, and Examples."

5. "The Global Haves and Have-Nots in the 21st Century," ineteconomics.org, November 15, 2015.

6. "The Global Haves and Have-Nots in the 21st Century."

7. "The Global Haves and Have-Nots in the 21st Century."

8. Cheryl Russell, *The Master Trend: How the Baby Boom Generation is Remaking America* (New York: Plenum, 1993), 56–57.

9. "Leading with Customer-Focused Content: Driving Growth Through Personalized Experiences," *Forbes Insights*, January 2016, 2.

10. Lydia A. Clougherty Jones, "Leveraging Data in a Personalized Economy: From Insights to Income," linkedin.com, July 24, 2016.

11. Melanie Swan, "Personalized Economic Systems: Self-Determination and Economic Theory," ieet.org, August 20, 2015.

12. Daniel Dickson, "Swedish Central Bank Eyeing E-Currency," reuters.com, November 16, 2016.

13. Wendy McElroy, "Fedcoin: The U.S. Will Issue E-Currency That You Will Use," news.bitcoin.com, January 12, 2017.

14. Jeremy Gaunt, "Cashless Society Getting Closer, Survey Finds," reuters.com, April 26, 2017.

15. "Bitcoin: The History of Money and the Future of Digital Currency," nuskool.com, June 11, 2015.

16. Homi Kharas, "Global Middle-Class Growth Will Drive the World Economy," thehill.com, March 10, 2017.

17. Kharas, "Global Middle-Class Growth Will Drive the World Economy."

18. Homi Kharas, "How a Growing Global Middle Class Could Save the World's Economy," magazine-aws.pewtrusts.org, July 5, 2016.

19. Kharas, "How a Growing Global Middle Class Could Save the World's Economy."

20. Beth Novitsky, "Microbrands: Think Small," gensleron.com, November 18, 2015.

21. Novitsky, "Microbrands."

22. Kevin Gaughan and Dan Rottenberg, "Microbranding Leads to Big Success," retaillawadvisor.com, May 11, 2016.

23. Billee Howard, "The Rise of Microbrands and Why Bigger Isn't Better Anymore," brandthropologie.com.

24. Faisal Hoque, "How the Rising Gig Economy is Reshaping Businesses," fastcompany.com, September 22, 2015.

25. "Map: Entrepreneurship Around the World," blog.approvedindex.co.uk.

26. Hoque, "How the Rising Gig Economy is Reshaping Businesses."

27. Slava Solodkiy, "'Gig' Economy Is on the Rise," medium.com, February 20, 2017.

28. Solodkiy, "'Gig' Economy Is on the Rise."

29. Paul Morin, "How Not to Be a Victim of the Disintermediation Trend," companyfounder.com, June 8, 2107.

30. Morin, "How Not to Be a Victim."

31. Morin, "How Not to Be a Victim."

32. Rachel Croson, "The Future of Business is Disintermediated," linkedin.com, January 19, 2016.

33. Kate, "E-Commerce Sales in the US Made up Just 8% of Total Retail Sales in Q1 2016," letstalkpayments.com, June 28, 2016.

34. Kate, "E-Commerce Sales in the US."

35. "National Retail Federation Estimates 8–12% US E-Commerce Growth in 2017," businessinsider.com, February 10, 2017.

36. Jason Trout, "5 Excellent Examples of Omnichannel Retailing Done Right," multichannelmerchant.com, February 2, 2017.

37. Saad Khan, "Future of E-Commerce: Five Trends to Watch Out For in 2017," entrepreneur.com, May 7, 2017.

38. Sophie Shimansky, "The Return of Analog," dw.com, April 11, 2017.

39. Shimansky, "The Return of Analog."

40. Suzanne Cords, "Young Artists Find Inspiration in Pre-Digital Age," dw.com, July 23, 2014.

41. David Sax, *The Revenge of Analog: Real Things and Why They Matter* (New York: Public Affairs, 2016).

Chapter 3. Political Trends

1. "Geopolitical Instability," thefuturescentre.org, November 9, 2015.

2. "Geopolitical Instability."

3. Ian Bremmer, "The Top 5 Geopolitical Risks for 2016," time.com, January 7, 2016.

4. "Geostrategic Risks on the Rise," mckinsey.com, May 2016.

5. Pippa Norris, "It's Not Just Trump," washingtonpost.com, March 11, 2016.

6. National Intelligence Council, "Global Trends: Paradox of Progress," January 2017, 17–18.

7. Norris, "It's Not Just Trump."

8. Matt McFarland, "Trump's Populism is Only the Beginning," money.cnn.com, November 17, 2016.

9. Heather Hurlburt and Chayenne Polimedio, "Can Transpartisan Coalitions Overcome Polarization?" newamerica.org, May 16, 2016.

10. "The Party of the Future," policy-network.net.

11. Peter Drucker, *The Age of Discontinuity: Guidelines to Our Changing Society* (Oxford, UK: Butterworth-Heinemann, 1969).

12. W. P. S. Sidhu, "Global Trends: Discontinuities and Disruption—Risks and Challenges for the World," *Mint*, January 16, 2017.

13. Klaus Schwab, *The Global Risks Report 2017*, 12th ed. (Geneva: World Economic Forum, 2017), 4.

14. Steven Konkoly, *Rogue State* (Seattle: Thomas & Mercer, 2017).

15. "The Concept of a Rogue State Politics Essay," ukessays.com, March 23, 2015.

16. "A Working Definition of E-Government," ctg.albany.edu.

17. Sten Tamkivi, "Lessons from the World's Most Tech-Savvy Government," theatlantic.com, January 24, 2014.

18. "Working Definition of E-Government."

19. "Working Definition of E-Government."

20. Hana Francisco and Carly Olson, "E-Government and E-Politics in the United States," prezi.com, May 24, 2011.

21. Joshua Habursky and Mike Fulton, "The Future of Politics is Grassroots," thehill.com, March 12, 2017.

22. Habursky and Fulton, "The Future of Politics is Grassroots."

23. James Badcock, "How the New Digital Grassroots is Reshaping Politics," shapingthefuture.economist.com.

24. Chrystia Freeland, "The Disintegration of the World," theatlantic.com, May 2015.

25. Peter Turchin, *Ages of Discord: A Structural-Demographic Analysis of American History* (Storrs, CT: Beresta, 2016).

26. Charles W. Kegley and Shannon L. Blanton, *World Politics: Trend and Transformation, 2014–2015* (Boston: Cengage Learning, 2014), 210.

27. Freeland, "The Disintegration of the World."

28. Matthew Wood, "Why 'Anti-Politics' is Not a Myth," policy-network.net, October 28, 2014.

29. Peter Barnett, "What is Green Politics?" greenworld.org.uk, January 16, 2015.

30. Barnett, "What is Green Politics?"

31. Jedediah Purdy, "Green Politics Has to Get More Radical, Because Anything Less is Impractical," thedailybeast.com, April 26, 2014.

Chapter 4. Social Trends

1. Mike Fromowitz, "Muticulturalism: The Unstoppable Global Trend," campaignasia.com, July 31, 2014.

2. "America's Tipping Point: Most of U.S. Now Multicultural, Says Group," nbcnews.com, August 22, 2014.

3. "The New Mainstream," ethnifacts.com.

4. "The New Mainstream."

5. "Special Report: The Family Structure of the Future," blog.euromonitor.com, July 5, 2013.

6. "Special Report: The Family Structure of the Future."

7. "Special Report: The Family Structure of the Future."

8. George Gao, "Americans' Ideal Family Size is Smaller Than It Used To Be," pewresearch.org, May 8, 2015.

9. "Urbanization on the Rise—Trends, Challenges, the Road Ahead," urbanhub.com.

10. "Urbanization on the Rise."

11. "Urbanization Trends in 2020: Mega Cities and Smart Cities Built on a Vision of Sustainability," frost.com.

12. "Urbanization Trends in 2020."

13. Molly Wood, "Co-living Startups: The Commune is Back, But for Profit," marketplace.com, June 2, 2016.

14. Jenny Southan, "Why Co-Living is Transforming the Way We Work and Travel," globetrendermagazine.com, January 8, 2017.

15. Lucy Ingham, "The Co-Living Revolution is Coming, and this is its Blueprint," factor-tech.com, April 28, 2016.

16. Southan, "Why Co-Living is Transforming the Way We Work and Travel."

17. Melia Robinson, "Millennials are Paying Thousands of Dollars a Month for Maid Service and Instant Friends in 'Hacker Houses,'" businessinsider.com, March 8, 2017.

18. Robinson, "Millennials are Paying Thousands."

19. Ingham, "Co-Living Revolution is Coming."

20. Peter G. Peterson, *Grey Dawn: How the Coming Age Wave Will Transform America—and the World* (New York: Crown, 1999), 5.

21. census.gov.

22. Val Srinivas and Urval Goradia, "The Future of Wealth in the United States," dupress.deloitte.com, November 9, 2015.

23. "Introducing Boomers: Marketing's Most Valuable Generation," nielsen.com, August 6, 2012.

24. Lawrence R. Samuel, *Boomers 3.0: Marketing to Baby Boomers in Their Third Act of Life* (Santa Barbara, CA: Praeger, 2017).

25. Samuel, *Boomers 3.0*.

26. Samuel, *Boomers 3.0.*

27. Nicole McGougan, "Survey Says! Boomers Dominate Charitable Giving," trust.guidestar.org, August 15, 2013.

28. Allison Pond, "Baby Boomers are About to Give $8 Trillion to Charity, but They Won't Just Write a Check," deseretnews.com, March 2, 2016.

29. Samuel, *Boomers 3.0.*

30. "'This is the Century of the Woman,' Deputy Secretary-General Says, Urging Conference to Strive towards Full, Equal Participation in Society," un.org, September 23, 2014.

31. Christopher Barnatt, "More Women in Authority," explainingthefuture.com, September 24, 2012.

32. "Intuit 2020 Report," October 2010, intuit.com.

33. "It's a She-conomy," sheconomy2020.com.

34. Dan Fennessy, "The Next Tech Trend: Real Human Connection," medium.com, March 19, 2017.

35. Fennessy, "Next Tech Trend."

36. Fennessy, "Next Tech Trend."

37. Shoshanna Delventhal, "Baby Boomer Philanthropy Shifts Wealth Adviser Focus," investopedia.com, October 7, 2015.

38. Jennifer Woods, "Doing Well While Doing Good: Socially Responsible Investing," cnbc.com, September 24, 2015.

39. Kevin Mahn, "The Changing Face of Socially Responsible Investing," forbes.com, April 26, 2016.

40. Scott Stanley, "Socially Responsible Investing: Aligning Investments and Values," linkedin.com, January 14, 2016.

41. Vikram Alexei Kansara, "How Global Brands Are Thinking Local," businessoffashion.com, July 4, 2016.

42. Kansara, "How Global Brands Are Thinking Local."

Chapter 5. Scientific Trends

1. Matt Burgess, "Future of Space Exploration: Drones, Submarines and Self-Replicating Robots," factor-tech.com, February 10, 2015.

2. Burgess, "Future of Space Exploration."

3. George Whitesides, "Where Will Space Technology Take Us by 2030, and What Does This Mean for Life on Earth?" weforum.org, February 22, 2017.

4. Whitesides, "Where Will Space Technology Take Us by 2030?"

5. Cheyenne Macdonald, "Will an AI be the First to Find Alien Life? NASA Backs Plans for Smart Robotic Explorers That Could Scour the Universe," dailymail.co.uk, June 22, 2017.

6. Nikhil Krishnan, "Genomics 101: Understanding How the Genomics Revolution is Changing Medicine," cbinsights.com, November 10, 2016.

7. Krishnan, "Genomics 101."

8. Enakshi Singh, "A Look Ahead: Seven Trends Shaping Genomics in 2017 and Beyond," genengnews.com, December 29, 2016.

9. 23andme.com.

10. Lavinia Ionita, "Innovation in Genomics and the Future of Medtech," techcrunch.com, April 20, 2016, omixy.com.

11. "Climate Geoengineering—Experimenting with the Global Thermostat," boell.de, March 16, 2017.

12. "Climate Geoengineering."

13. Arthur Neslen, "US Scientists Launch World's Biggest Solar Geoengineering Study," theguardian.com, March 24, 2017.

14. Neslen, "US Scientists Launch World's Biggest Solar Geoengineering Study."

15. "What Does Longevity Mean for Future Generations?" focusingfuture.com.

16. "What Does Longevity Mean for Future Generations?"

17. Gregg Easterbrook, "What Happens When We All Live to 100?" theatlantic.com, October 2014.

18. nano.gov.

19. Niamh Louise Marriott, "Predictions for the Future: How Nanoscience Will Improve Our Health and Lives," drugtargetreview.com, October 27, 2016.

20. Marriott, "Predictions for the Future."

21. Alan Brown, "The Future of Nanoscience: Three Kavli Nanoscience Institute Directors Forecast the Field's Future," kavlifoundation.org, Winter 2014.

22. Evelyne Celerier, "The Past, Present and Future of Neuroscience Research," laboratoryequipment.com, January 6, 2017.

23. Gary Marcus, "A Map for the Future of Neuroscience," newyorker.com, September 17, 2013.

24. Marcus, "A Map for the Future of Neuroscience."

25. Marcus, "A Map for the Future of Neuroscience."

26. Kayt Sukel, "Big Data and the Brain: Peeking at the Future of Neuroscience," dana.org, November 30, 2015.

27. Earl Lane, "Neuroscience's Future Includes Medical Advances and Ethical Quandaries," aaas.org, November 25, 2014.

28. Bahar Gholipour, "'The Future of the Brain': A Time Capsule of Neuroscience," livescience.com, December 15, 2014.

29. REN21, "Renewables Global Futures Report: Great Debates Towards 100% Renewable Energy," 2017.

30. REN21, "Renewables Global Futures Report."

31. "Renewable Energy Can Provide 80 Percent of U.S. Electricity by 2050," ucsusa.org.

32. Leslie Kaufman, "How New York Is Building the Renewable Energy Grid of the Future," insideclimatenews.org, May 25, 2017.

33. "Sustainability Science," unesco.org.

34. Benjamin P. Warner, "Sustainability is a New Academic Discipline. But Is It Sustainable?" theconversation.com, September 21, 2015.

35. Warner, "Sustainability is a New Academic Discipline."

36. Warner, "Sustainability is a New Academic Discipline."

37. Kennedy School of Government, "About Us," hks.harvard.edu.

38. Jay Keasling, "Why Synthetic Biology is the Field of the Future," pbs.org, February 28, 2013.

39. Keasling, "Why Synthetic Biology is the Field of the Future."

40. gingkobioworks.com.

41. Michael Eisenstein, "Living Factories of the Future," nature.com, March 17, 2016.

42. Angela Chen, "How to Create a New Life Form: Historian Sophia Roosth on the Future of Synthetic Biology," theverge.com, April 4, 2017.

43. Zoltan Istvan, "Are You Ready for the Future of Transhumanism?" huffingtonpost.com, May 31, 2016.

44. Istvan, "Are You Ready for the Future of Transhumanism?"

45. Marcelo Gleiser, "The Transhuman Future: Be More Than You Can Be," npr.org, June 11, 2014.

46. Karla Lant, "The Future of the Human Brain: Smart Drugs and Nootropics," futurism.com, April 10, 2017.

47. Lant, "The Future of the Human Brain."

Chapter 6. Technological Trends

1. Elizabeth Kolbert, "Our Automated Future," newyorker.com, December 19 & 26, 2016.

2. Kolbert, "Our Automated Future."

3. Richard Gray, "How Automation Will Affect You—The Experts' View," bbc.com, May 23, 2017.

4. Gray, "How Automation Will Affect You."

5. Peter Miscovich, "The Future is Automated. Here's How We Can Prepare For It," weforum.org, January 12, 2017.

6. Larry Alton, "A Look at the Latest Trends in Biometric Tech," itproportal.com, May 16, 2017.

7. Alton, "A Look at the Latest Trends."

8. Alton, "A Look at the Latest Trends."

9. Danny Thakkar, "10 Biometric Technology Trends to Watch in 2017," bayometric.com, February 8, 2017.

10. "Connectivity and Convergence—Connected Living," ww2.frost.com.

11. investinbsr.com.

12. "Convergence to Define New Business Models in the Future, Says Frost & Sullivan," ww2.frost.com, March 2, 2015.

13. "Convergence to Define New Business Models."

14. Richard van Hooijdonk, "The 7 Technology Trends That Will Dominate the Future," richardvanhooijdonk.com, January 26, 2016.

15. van Hooijdonk, "7 Technology Trends."

16. "About the Cognitive Horizons Network," research.ibm.com.

17. "A Computer Called Watson," http://www-03.ibm.com.

18. Scott Corwin, Nick Jameson, Derek M. Pankratz, and Philipp Willigmann, "The Future of Mobility: What's Next?" dupress.deloitte.com, September 14, 2016.

19. Corwin, Jameson, Pankratz, and Willigmann, "The Future of Mobility."

20. Corwin, Jameson, Pankratz, and Willigmann, "The Future of Mobility."

21. Thomas H. Davenport, "A Predictive Analytics Primer," hbr.org, September 2, 2014.

22. "What is Predictive Analytics?" predictiveanalyticstoday.com.

23. "What is Predictive Analytics?"

24. "Predictive Analytics: What It is and Why It Matters," sas.com.

25. Grant Stanley, "Diapers, Beer, and Data Science in Retail," canworksmart.com, July 17, 2012.

26. *Quantum Leap*, en.wikipedia.org.

27. Amy Webb, "8 Tech Trends to Watch in 2016," hbr.org, December 8. 2015.

28. Jeremy O'Brien, "The Future is Quantum," ft.com, March 24, 2017.

29. O'Brien, "Future is Quantum."

30. Kelly Dickerson, "7 Awesome Ways Quantum Computers Will Change the World," businessinsider.com, April 21, 2015.

31. Dickerson, "7 Awesome Ways."

32. Jen Quinlan, "The Future of Wearable Tech," wired.com, February 2015.

33. Quinlan, "Future of Wearable Tech."

34. Quinlan, "Future of Wearable Tech."

35. Amy Forni, "The Present and Future of Wearables," gartner.com, December 16, 2016.

36. van Hooijdonk, "7 Technology Trends."

37. Nelson Kunkel and Steve Soechtig, "Mixed Reality: Experiences Get More Intuitive, Immersive, and Empowering," dupress.deloitte.com, January 7, 2017.

38. Kunkel and Soechtig, "Mixed Reality."

39. Kunkel and Soechtig, "Mixed Reality."

40. Howard Lear, "Technological Singularity: What's the Future of Artificial Intelligence?" clicksoftware.com, January 18, 2016.

41. Lear, "Technological Singularity."

42. Patrick Caughill, "Ray Kurzweil's Most Exciting Predictions about the Future of Humanity," futurism.com, June 5, 2017.

43. Drake Baer, "9 Crazy Things That Could Happen After the Singularity, When Robots Become Smarter Than Humans," businessinsider.com, December 18, 2015.

~

Selected Bibliography

Coyne, Jerry A. *Faith Versus Fact: Why Science and Religion Are Incompatible*. New York: Viking, 2015.

Drucker, Peter. *The Age of Discontinuity: Guidelines to Our Changing Society*. Oxford, UK: Butterworth-Heinemann, 1969.

Kegley, Charles W., and Shannon L. Blanton. *World Politics: Trend and Transformation, 2014–2015*. Boston: Cengage Learning, 2014.

Peterson, Peter G. *Grey Dawn: How the Coming Age Wave Will Transform America—and the World*. New York: Crown, 1999.

Pine, Joseph, and James Gilmore. *The Experience Economy: Work is Theater & Every Business a Stage*. Cambridge, MA: Harvard Business School Press, 1999.

Russell, Cheryl. *The Master Trend: How the Baby Boom Generation is Remaking America*. New York: Plenum, 1993.

Samuel, Lawrence R. *The American Way of Life: A Cultural History*. London: Fairleigh Dickinson University Press, 2017.

———. *Boomers 3.0: Marketing to Baby Boomers in Their Third Act of Life*. Santa Barbara, CA: Praeger, 2017.

Sandison, Alan, and Robert Dingley, ed. *Histories of the Future: Studies in Fact, Fantasy and Science Fiction*. New York: Palgrave, 2000.

Sax, David. *The Revenge of Analog: Real Things and Why They Matter*. New York: Public Affairs, 2016.

Schwartz, Barry. *The Paradox of Choice: Why More is Less*. New York: HarperCollins, 2004.

Taleb, Nassim Nicholas. *The Black Swan: The Impact of the Highly Improbable*. New York: Random House, 2007.

Turchin, Peter. *Ages of Discord: A Structural-Demographic Analysis of American History*. Storrs, CT: Beresta, 2016.

Wilson, David A. *The History of the Future*. Toronto: McArthur & Company, 2000.

Index

education: e-learning, 122; and
feminization, 119–21; and freelance
economy, 61–62; and global middle
class, 55; and microfamilies, 105; and
secularization, 14; and sustainability,
152–53; and urbanization, 108; and
virtuality, 184–87
electronics, 144, 182
energy: appetite for, 132; and climate
mitigation, 139; and convergence,
169; and deregulation, 43; and
disintermediation, 64; and ESG
investing, 125; and nanoscience,
143–44; and predictive analytics, 177;
and quantum computing, 179, 181;
renewable, 149–51; space-based solar
power, 168; and urbanization, 108
entertainment, 16, 26, 55, 106, 174,
184–87

Facebook, 16, 23, 54, 88, 90, 168
families, 48, 95, 102, 105–107, 124
fashion/clothing, 25–26, 66, 128, 144,
155, 182–84
food and beverages, 58, 63, 103, 127,
143–44, 155
Ford Motor, 174
fragrances, 155
futurism, 3–7, 101, 176–79

Geico, 63
General Motors, 174
Generation Z (post-millennial), 25–27,
60, 65, 70, 102
Google, 136, 141, 168, 179
government: and biometrics, 165–
67; decline of, 18, 93, 96; and
deregulation, 42–44; and e-currency,
51–52; e-government, 87–88; gender
gaps in, 119; and grassroots activism,
90; local, 82, 84, 110; and populism,
14, 75
"Greatest Generation," 14, 65

health care: and aging, 113–15; and
artificial intelligence, 171; and
automation, 163; and biometrics, 165;
and coalitions, 79; and convergence,
169; Eastern, 31–32; genomics,
135–37; and global middle class, 55;
health span, 141–43; personalized,
49–50, 135; and predictive analytics,
177; and quantum computing, 179,
181; and urbanization, 108; and
wearables, 182–84
Hello Fresh, 63
Hewlett-Packard, 179
homes, 60, 64, 110–13, 161, 168
hospitality, 185
household products, 144

IBM, 136, 171–72, 179
insurance, 177, 183
Intel, 136
investing, 124–27

Jaguar Land Rover, 166
J.P. Morgan, 125

Kickstarter, 63

legal, 163
lululemon, 128

McDonald's, 161
media, 57, 63
medicine: and artificial intelligence,
190; and biometrics, 165; Eastern,
31–32; genomics, 135–37; and
longevity, 141; and marijuana,
28; and nanoscience, 143–44; and
neuroscience, 146; personalized,
50; and pharmacopeia, 29; and
predictive analytics, 177; and
synthetic biology, 154–55; and
transhumanism, 157–59; and
wearables, 182–83

~

About the Author

Lawrence (Larry) R. Samuel is the founder of AmeriCulture, a consultancy based out of Miami and New York City that is dedicated to translating the emerging cultural landscape into business opportunities. Called "the Margaret Mead of plutocrats" by Slate.com, Larry has been a leading culture consultant to Fortune 500 companies and blue-chip advertising agencies since 1990. As one of the top trend consultants in the country, he advised a Who's Who of companies and agencies across a wide variety of industries and categories, including Anheuser-Busch, Baskin-Robbins, Chase, Condé Nast, General Mills, Hasbro, John Hancock, Liberty Mutual, L. L. Bean, and Whirlpool. Larry's breakthrough research study on American wealth culture for J. P. Morgan, which identified five types of American millionaires based on his unique methodology rooted in cultural anthropology, was widely reported in the media. Larry is a blogger for *Psychology Today*, where he has received hundreds of thousands of hits. He holds a PhD in American Studies from the University of Minnesota and is the author of many books, including *The Future Ain't What It Used to Be: The 40 Cultural Trends Transforming Your Job, Your Life, Your World* (1998), *Future: A Recent History* (2009), *Rich: The Rise and Fall of American Wealth Culture* (2009), and *Boomers 3.0: Marketing to Baby Boomers in Their Third Act of Life* (2017).